REACHING FOR THE SKY

A Challenge to Young Adulthood

THOMAS B. PITMAN III

PATHWAY PRESS
Cleveland, Tennessee

Library of Congress Catalog Card Number: 75-37358
International Standard Book Number: 0-87148-731-4

To Mary
my wife . . .
sweetheart . . .
constant companion . . .
and closest friend

CONTENTS

ACKNOWLEDGMENTS

Writing this book developed into a far greater task than I had anticipated. I knew it would take time, energy, lots of research, and much work. I was right; but it took much more than I thought. It would have been impossible except for the help and support of many.

Much credit has to go to Dr. James D. Williams of Southwestern Baptist Theological Seminary, Fort Worth, Texas, who first introduced me to the needs of a ministry in adult education. My wife, Mary, deserves much more than her name on the dedication page. She has helped with the research, the typing, and the editing and, most of all, with a super amount of encouragement. Tammy, Benjy, Cary, and Joy—my wonderful children—have been more than understanding in allowing their daddy to spend much of his time on a book—time that, by rights, should have been spent with them. Aroma Kemp was of invaluable help in the final stages with the typing.

I cannot express enough of my appreciation to the congregation of the Edgewater Church of God, Denver, Colorado, who have been more than understanding, supportive, encouraging, and patient as their pastor carried the burden for this book. I trust the finished book justifies their patience and concern.

—THOMAS B. PITTMAN III

1

BECOMING A YOUNG ADULT

Unlike the periods of childhood and youth, the period of young adulthood is not easily defined. Age alone is not the only criterium, as young adulthood is also typified by certain developmental tasks.

Young adulthood has always, evidently, been a trying time. Paul, writing to Timothy, a young adult, says in 1 Timothy 4:12, "Let no man despise thy youth." Or, as J. B. Phillips translates it, "Don't let people look down on you because you are young."

The Times of Young Adulthood

Earl F. Zeigler, in *Christian Education of Adults,* says, "Adulthood begins when life compels growing persons to accept adult responsibilities." It is impossible to classify young adults strictly by age. When a simple age criterium is used, generally young adults are said to be between eighteen and twenty-nine years of age. Some, however, consider young adulthood to continue through age forty.

It is much easier to use other means than just age to determine young adulthood. The persons in this age-group vary greatly. Thomas R. Bennett, writing in the December, 1965, issue of *International Journal of Religious Education,* gives a breakdown of young adulthood in this way:

—Some are single, but more are married;

—Some are dropouts; others have completed their high school education and gone to college, or have years of college work ahead;

—Some are teenage young marrieds and parents; others in their late twenties are single; and

—Four out of ten have been in their present job less than one year, and over half receive incomes of less than $3,500 a year.

Young adulthood is characterized as being one of the loneliest periods of life. It is marked by a desire to go one's own way, but also to go that way with the friends and acquaintances of one's own choosing.

Yet, at the same time, it is a period when the individual, or at most two individuals, must face and decide on some of the most important and crucial issues of life.

Elizabeth B. Hurlock, in *Developmental Psychology,* describes this time as the reproductive age, the settling-down age, the problem age, and the age of great emotional tension. This period in life normally includes getting married, permanently leaving home, completing one's formal schooling, becoming self-supporting, reaching one's political majority, entering military service, and attaining a certain chronological age that says to the world, "I am an adult." Further, at the time the young adult is facing all these events, he is by personality feeling liberated, skeptical, and searching.

Today the young adult finds himself in a social environment for which there is no precedent. This adds to his feeling of frustration. This also emphasizes his drastic need to find a deep-founded faith in God.

The words of the writer of Hebrews seem appropriate to the young adult: "Keep your lives free from the lust for money: be content with what you have. God has said: I will in no wise fail thee, Neither will I in any wise forsake thee. We, therefore, can confidently say: The Lord is my helper; I will not fear: What shall man do unto me?" (Hebrews 13:5, 6; *Phillips*).

The Development Tasks of Young Adulthood

Most authorities on young adulthood agree that there are eight developmental tasks with which the young adult must cope. These eight tasks are choosing a mate, learning to live with a marriage partner, starting a family, rearing children, managing a home, getting started in an occupation, taking on civic responsibility, and finding a congenial social group. As Christians we would add another, the most important of all: finding a vibrant faith for living. This one will, when accomplished, help all of the other ones to fall into their proper perspective. The Apostle Paul said, "I can do all things through Christ which strengtheneth me" (Philippians 4:13). A young adult needs that kind of vibrant faith and confidence in Christ as he approaches his tasks.

Lewis Joseph Sherrill, in *Struggle of the Soul,* suggests that the central task of young adulthood is making the basic identification around which life as a mature adult can be developed. He identifies this period of life as the time when the philosophy of living is, "Get as much as you can and give as little in return as you can get away with."

So these are the tasks facing the young adult. They provide a multitude of possible teaching situations for the church. Further, God gives the church authority to teach and train young adults in all areas of living (1 Peter 5:5). And yet, as quoted earlier, this is the time of life when the least amount of teaching is done.

Robert J. Havighurst, in his book *Human Development and Education,* points out that this period of life, from eighteen to thirty, usually contains marriage, the first pregnancy, the first serious full-time job, the first illnesses of children, the first experience of furnishing or buying or building a house, and the first venture of sending the child off to school. If ever there is a time when people are ready and motivated to learn, he points out, it is during times such as these.

And though meager help, if any, is offered by

various secular agencies, the average church offers no teaching, counsel, or direction in these areas. And yet, many wonder why the average young adult is not interested in church. The reason should be obvious. The church is not meeting his needs, and he considers church involvement irrelevant to this particular time in his life.

The Handicaps of Meeting Those Tasks

The young adult is also faced with a variety of handicaps or hindrances to accomplishing these developmental tasks. One of these handicaps is urbanization.

Marvin J. Taylor, in *Introduction to Christian Education,* says: "The urban revolution has led to the breaking down of community, the crumbling of traditions and values, the rapidity of social change, the diversity of adult models, the changing function of the family, and the increased mobility of the young. With few certainties and almost no guidelines, the process of becoming adult has become more difficult, the crises more pronounced, and the time required to complete the tasks more specified."

Mass media also is a handicap as well as an aid in the realm of meeting needs. There are educational programs available to help prepare the young adult to meet needs; but, at the same time, if he allows television to absorb too much of his time, he is wasting time which would have been better spent if he had done his tasks. Too many families sit and watch television so much that they never really learn the art of communicating. Daytime soap operas (where everyone is divorcing and where extramarital affairs run rampant) also are a bad influence; they handicap young adults who are trying to establish a happy, well-balanced home.

Another handicap is the lack of effort by any one institution to minister to all areas of the young adult's life. One institution will emphasize the spiritual, another the vocational, still another the social, and so on. We rarely find one institution that ministers to all the needs of the young adult.

The church is the logical one to help here. It should be more than a Sunday meeting place. It should equip the young adult with the spiritual values necessary to confront every area of his life and to meet the tasks before him.

God is concerned about all areas of one's life. This will include vocational guidance, in-depth premarriage counseling, child-rearing, and many other areas in which the church should offer assistance. When the various institutions, including the church, fail to reach more than one part of his life, the young adult never sees his life as a whole, but only as fragmented parts. He concludes that there is, therefore, no carry-over from work to school to church to home.

The church must help him realize that these are not separates, but are, in fact, very related and that all must fit together in a logical, consistent way or he is in for some very trying emotional experiences. Unfortunately, most churches fail miserably

in the area of ministering to all areas of the young
adult's life.

In *Developmental Psychology* Elizabeth B. Hurlock lists four handicaps to mastering developmental tasks:

1. *Discontinuities in training—*

   *The training and schooling given to chil-
   dren and youth does not relate to the pattern of life in adulthood. Only when an
   older student takes a course of study in
   some professional area is there any con-
   tinuity to what he is studying and what
   he is going to need to know.*

2. *Overprotectiveness—*

   *Americans have a tendency to overprotect
   their children and shield them from many
   learning situations. We don't want to cause
   them unhappiness so we try and shield
   them from disappointments and hardships.
   Parental overprotectiveness can result in a
   child so dependent that he is totally unprepared for and unable to function as a
   young adult.*

3. *Prolongation of peer-group influences—*

   *By the time a person goes through high
   school and college, he has spent 16 years
   in his peer-group. Thus he is very dependent on peer-group attitudes and values.
   The longer the education, the longer one
   tends to stay in his peer-group. When
   his education is complete, and he is thrust*

fully into society as a young adult on his own, problems can result.

4. *Unrealistic aspirations—*
   Trying to reach a goal set by a parent or trying to become something simply out of his reach can be terribly frustrating and can become a handicap in accomplishing his tasks.

These are some of the handicaps young adults face in trying to master their developmental tasks.

The Concerns and Needs of Young Adults

The things that concern young adults are intensely personal. This period of life finds people very self-centered, seeking ways to promote their own welfare.

Early adulthood is a time of storm and stress in America, and particularly in the middle-class part of American society, according to Robert J. Havighurst in *Human Development and Education.* The reason, he points out, is that the young adult is going from an age-graded society to a society graded on social status. In the adult society prestige and power depend not so much on age as they did in childhood and youth, but on skill, strength, wisdom, and family connections.

Here the Christian has the greatest advantage: he can draw from a great strength and wisdom that the world knows nothing about. Look at James 1:5 and Ephesians 6:10. Who has greater family connections than the Christian? No one! Achieving the goals of life are not simply a matter now of a person's waiting until he is of proper age, as before, but a matter of his ability to achieve and perform.

Another concern of the young adult is his changing interest. He is reassessing his old interests to see if they fit into his new life-style. He is assessing them in regard to money, time, companionship, and physical strength and energy needed to carry them out.

Earl F. Zeigler, in *Christian Education of Adults*, suggests eight areas of concern to the young adult: vocation, use of leisure time, life goals, emotional growth and security, sex life and mating, family responsibility and conflicts, pressures of a changing culture, and religious and spiritual growth. Realizing that young adults are concerned about all these phases of life, the church must cease to work solely in the latter area and start to help young adults to satisfactorily meet all eight areas.

A major concern of young adults who are church-oriented is that they do not seem to fit into the program of many local churches. Especially single young adults or divorced or widowed young adults feel totally lost in the average church. Most churches are family oriented. They have family-night suppers and educational programs geared to children and couples.

But these have little or no appeal to the single young adult. It is no wonder that most single young adults learn that they can get along without the church. Once they are away from home, they are not eager to lift the phone and call the nearest church to find out about services. Feeling that the church is somewhat unconcerned about their needs and interests, they generally adopt a "wait and see" attitude.

Marvin J. Taylor, author of *Introduction to Christian Education*, suggests eight other areas of concern to young adults:

1. *Problem of anomie or being detached, disorganized, ungoverned, and uncommitted.*

2. *Problem of poor mental health caused by the unusually high level of guilt and anxiety found in many young adults. . . . Depression, guilt and wishful thinking increase in the twenties.*

3. *Marital problems and divorce are urgent concerns of young adults. The greatest stress in marriage usually occurs during the first five years.*

4. *Almost every study points to sex as a major concern of young adults.*

5. *Crime and delinquency involve a limited number of persons in our society, but this is ever increasing, especially among young adults. This age group makes up the majority of state and federal prisoners and commits the highest rate of hard core crime.*

6. *The problem of mobility is actually more symptomatic of the problem of rootlessness. It does indicate how difficult it is for society to maintain contact with this transi-*

tional group. At least 40 percent of men
and women under thirty-five are reported
to change addresses every year.

7. The problem of unemployment is a major
concern of young adults. There are more
workers than jobs unless educated and
trained.

8. The concern over the stigma attached to
the unmarried young adult especially
when social success is measured in terms of
marriage.

Young adults know that they have critical needs
and will respect and welcome competent and mature attempts to counsel and help them. The
church willing to do so will find young adults
waiting.

Summary

Young adulthood is one of the major adjustment
times in life. Most young adults face this time
tragically unprepared. Because of this, a great deal
of experimenting and mistake-making occurs during this time. Young adults want to learn and can
adjust and change. The church has an obligation
to help its young adults meet the tasks of this life
period.

The remaining chapters will deal with some of
the individual areas of young adulthood in more
detail.

2

HANDLING EMOTIONAL STRESS

The period of young adulthood is one of the most emotionally tense periods of life. The pressures of succeeding in college or learning a trade, the pressure of succeeding in one's chosen vocation, the pressure of succeeding in marriage, and a host of other pressures cause this to be a particularly tense and emotional period of life.

Causes of Stress

It has already been pointed out that in young adulthood a very quick and drastic change is made from an age-graded society to a status-graded society. During childhood and adolescence one progresses by gaining new freedoms and privileges based entirely on coming of age. He climbs the age ladder, gaining new privileges with each rung, until suddenly and abruptly he reaches young adulthood and runs out of rungs. Suddenly he must produce or else. He is now in a new and strange environment where he can advance only if he can discover the know-how needed to be successful.

Robert Havighurst, in *Human Development and Education,* points out that prestige and power depend no longer on age but on skill, strength, wisdom, and family connections. This is new to the young adult and most likely it will take several years for him to develop a strategy for conquering this new land. He must scout it out and decide how to survive in it.

Emotional stress is very strong during this time. While deciding on what vocation to enter, what college to attend, whom to marry, where to live, etc., the young adult is likely to be very tense and emotionally involved. During all of his life prior to this, he was geared to asking for help and receiving guidance from parents, school teachers, and church leaders. Now, facing the greatest decisions of life, in most cases, he is expected to go it alone. He goes without the supervision, guidance, or help that he had from his parents and teachers when he was younger. Now, his parents, many times, expect him to make his own decisions because he is supposedly mature. Because of his new freedom, the young adult, at times, is too proud to go to anyone else for help.

Also emotional stress results when aspirations and goals are set too high. If his goals are not matched by equal achievements, the young adult becomes, in Havighurst's words, a "climber." He thus begins to overstrive and overstrain in an effort to live up to his goals and aspirations. If his goals have been forced upon him by parents or peers, and are really not his own, this adds increased tension and possible resentment. All this can lead to an emotional breakdown and serious problems.

Emotional tension is often expressed in worries. What the young adult worries about will depend on what problems and adjustments he finds himself encountering at the moment and the degree of success or failure he is having. Havighurst says, "Money worries, for example, reach their peak at around age thirty, the time when economic problems in business and home life reach their peak. Worries about personal appearance, sexual morality, and making a good impression when meeting people, all of which are directly or indirectly related to courtship and finding a life mate, are most common during the early twenties. After thirty, worries center around health, making a success in business, and job security; as middle-age approaches, marital difficulties and family-relationship problems come to the fore."

By the time a young adult reaches thirty, generally he has settled into a life-style and pattern that he will stay with for life. His emotional tension begins to subside during this time as he has begun to solve most of these problems. Stability and calm begin to replace his former worries.

Solutions to Stress

The young adult must meet the challenge of the new arena of life in which he finds himself. He now must fight for himself and succeed on the basis of his skill and ability.

How does he do it? Generally, he scouts out the land. He tries to see what he has been thrust into and proceed from there. He experiments with different types of adjustments to his problems. The more scouting around he does, the more likely he is to come up with decisions that he can be happy with as he grows older.

The Church's Solution

It is unfair to allow young adults to tackle this time of stress alone. The church must communicate to its young adults that it cares and wants to help. Young adults need to realize that what they are going through is not unique to them. An atmosphere of love and understanding must be shown them especially during this time. Most importantly, the young adult must be led to understand that the Lord Jesus is interested in every area of his life.

God's Solution

God does not expect His children to be tense. In fact, worry is sin. To say that we believe that God loves us and takes care of all our needs, and then to worry about them, is wrong.

First Peter 5:7 gives us good counsel here: "[Cast] . . . all your care upon him; for he careth for you." God is not concerned with just our spiritual needs, but with every need we have.

Do you have problems on your job? Cast that problem on Jesus and let Him work it out. Why? Because He loves and cares for you. Are you carrying a financial burden? Cast it on Jesus, for He cares for you.

Most people fail in letting Jesus carry their burdens. They come to the Lord all bent over with care. The burden is supposedly cast upon the Lord, but then they walk away, still stooped and bent, still worrying.

Come to the Lord in faith believing. Put your burden upon Him, and then leave, standing straight and rejoicing that He has met your need. Remember: He cares for you!

J. B. Phillips' translation of Matthew 6:25-33 portrays the thought so beautifully:

> *That is why I say to you, Don't worry about living—wondering what you are going to eat or drink, or what you are going to wear. Surely life is more important than food, and the body more important than the clothes you wear. Look at the birds in the sky. They never sow nor reap nor store away in barns, and yet your Heavenly Father feeds them. Aren't you much more valuable to him than they are? Can any of you, however much he worries, make himself an inch taller? And why do you worry about clothes? Consider how the wild flowers grow. They neither*

work nor weave, but I tell you that even Solomon in all his glory was never arrayed like one of these! Now if God so clothes the flowers of the field, which are alive today and burned in the stove tomorrow, is he not much more likely to clothe you, you 'little-faiths'?

So don't worry and don't keep saying, 'What shall we eat, what shall we drink or what shall we wear?' That is what pagans are always looking for; your Heavenly Father knows that you need them all. Set your heart on his kingdom and his goodness, and all these things will come to you as a matter of course.

God is interested in His children not only spiritually, but also physically and mentally. He wants our physical and mental health to be just as good as our spiritual health.

"Dear friend, I pray that you may enjoy good health and that all may go well with you, even as your soul is getting along well" (3 John 1:2; *New International Version*). What John was saying is this: "I want you to prosper physically and mentally, even as you prosper spiritually."

Why then do people worry? Because they have a lack of faith in Christ's ability to meet their needs, or else a lack of understanding of what belongs to them in Christ Jesus. Jesus said in Mark 11:24: "Therefore I say unto you, What things soever ye desire, when ye pray, believe that ye receive them, and ye shall have them." This promise definitely includes victory over worry and emotional tension.

The Psalmist David knew this quiet and content place in God. In Psalm 18:1-3 he said, "I will love thee, O Lord, my strength. The Lord is my rock, and my fortress, and my deliverer; my God, my strength, in whom I will trust; my buckler, and the horn of my salvation, and my high tower. I will call upon the Lord, who is worthy to be praised: so shall I be saved from mine enemies." When the tasks at hand would cause us to worry, let us remember that the Lord cares for us and wants to carry our burdens.

How does one handle worry when the temptation comes to be concerned over something? Paul advised us here: "Casting down imaginations, and every high thing that exalteth itself against the knowledge of God, and bringing into captivity every thought to the obedience of Christ" (2 Corinthians 10:5).

This is pretty strong advice! We should bring every thought into obedience to Christ. What does that mean? It means that when we are tempted to worry, we should refuse to worry. We should put those thoughts away and bring our thoughts in line with the Word of God, which says that God cares for us and will meet our needs.

Paul treated this subject further in writing to the Roman Christians: "I beseech you therefore, brethren, by the mercies of God, that ye present your bodies a living sacrifice, holy, acceptable unto God, which is your reasonable service. And be not conformed to this world: but be ye transformed by the renewing of your mind, that ye may prove what is that good, and acceptable, and perfect, will of God" (Romans 12:1, 2).

How do we renew our minds? Through the Word of God. We should stop worrying about things we cannot change and start believing that God loves us and will meet our needs. We should commit our cares to Him.

David learned this lesson well. Toward the end of his life he penned these beautiful words:

The Lord is my shepherd; I shall not want. He maketh me to lie down in green pastures: he leadeth me beside the still waters. He restoreth my soul: he leadeth me in the paths of righteousness for his name's sake. Yea, though I walk through the valley of the shadow of death, I will fear no evil: for thou art with me; thy rod and thy staff they comfort me. Thou preparest a table before me in the presence of mine enemies: thou anointest my head with oil; my cup runneth over. Surely goodness and mercy shall follow me all the days of my life: and I will dwell in the house of the Lord for ever (Psalm 23:1-6).

Notice David's words: "I shall not want." "He restoreth my soul." "He leadeth me." "I will fear no evil." And on and on.

David had faith in his God. The young adult today, in the midst of the tensions and emotional pressures he faces, needs that same faith. It is up to the church to help him find it.

3

SETTING GOALS FOR LIVING

Too many people shoot for "nothing in particular in life" and hit it every time. Many young adults find themselves going nowhere and wondering why. They are like ships with no rudder: any wind carries them along. They do not know what they want or where they are going; nor do they have any idea of what they hope to accomplish when they get there.

This period of life, with all of the tensions already discussed in the previous chapter, becomes even more frustrating for the young adult with no goals or ambitions. The practice of sitting down, evaluating one's life, and deciding one's goals is fading. But the only way for a person to have a meaningful, satisfying, growing life is to know what he wants to do in life and to have goals for reaching it. Certainly, for the Christian this involves seeking the anointing and leading of the Holy Spirit.

Achieving Success

The meaning of *success* is ambiguous or, at the most, relative. According to the philosophy of the world, especially that portrayed through mass media advertising, *success* is "making money, driving an expensive car, and having certain things that denote achievement." But a man can have all of those things and not be successful, or have none of those things and be a success. Power, influence, and even honor are not necessarily signs of success. A man can rise to great heights and still make a big failure of his life.

Edward F. Garesche, in *The Will to Succeed,* says that "a successful life is a life that achieves its purpose." So a successful life has a purpose.

What is the purpose of your life? Have you ever sat down and thought about it?

Unfortunately, most people haven't. They are just living, taking things as they come, wondering why they do not see more happening in their lives. They plan to go nowhere, and wonder why they arrive! There will be mistakes and errors—no life is free of these. But, when we make a mistake, goals help us get back on track.

Garesche says, "The man who knows how to profit by his own errors is the one who makes a success of life. To be discouraged over your mistakes is foolish. To disregard them is equally unwise. To face them fearlessly and try to learn from them, how to avoid a mistake next time is the part of wisdom."

We have only a few years on this earth, and

we need to make those years meaningful. Knowing *what* we want to accomplish is a good part of successful living, and then accomplishing it comes next.

Finding Happiness

What does happiness have to do with success? Plenty.

Garesche describes *happiness* as "the inward contentment, the peace and satisfaction, the moral well being which comes to a man when he is a man, a real man, a man of prudence, justice, temperance, fortitude, a man who does his work and discharges his duty to God and his fellow beings."

Happiness is not necessarily pleasure. People around us are seeking pleasure, and thinking that in doing so they will find happiness. However, seeking pleasure, especially unlawful pleasure, simply ends in more frustration and turmoil. Pleasure, in itself, is not satisfying. It only leaves a craving for more. Happiness is deeper than this. Happiness comes from a life that knows where it is going and how it is going to get there.

The Bible speaks a great deal about happiness and joy. Joy is a fruit of the Spirit (Galatians 5: 22, 23). Nehemiah said that "the joy of the Lord is . . . [our] strength" (Nehemiah 8:10).

God wants us to be happy. That is not to say that we won't have valleys and trials, but we can be happy and successful if we are His children. If we simply float along in life—with no real goals, no real accomplishments—we get frustrated very quickly. But by setting our life on a course with carefully constructed goals and charted destinations, we are far more likely to be happy, because we are far more likely to be successful.

Living Positively

The Bible is very positive. Thus, Christian living should also be positive. We should know where we are going, because of the goals we have set; and, with a deep-seated faith in God, we should launch out to meet them. If we have a negative outlook on life, we will find ourselves in some rough water during young adulthood when there are so many important decisions to be made; but if we approach life positively, as a challenge we will have a much easier time.

Napoleon Hill spent twenty years studying the lives of some of the worlds most successful men and then wrote his book *Think and Grow Rich*. His major thrust was that all of the men he studied had a very positive attitude toward life. They did not dwell on negatives, things going wrong, or problems. Rather, they approached life by setting goals, by dwelling on the positive, by concentrating on things going right, by considering what they could do better, and so on. In approaching life very positively, Mr. Hill said, "every adversity, every failure, and every heartache carries with it the seed of an equivalent or a greater benefit."

He listed some major causes of failure:

Lack of a well-defined purpose in life
Lack of ambition to aim above mediocrity
Lack of self-discipline
Procrastination
Lack of persistence
Negative personality
Uncontrolled desire for "something for nothing"
Lack of a well-defined power of decision
Overcaution
Superstition and prejudice
Wrong selection of a vocation
Wrong selection of a mate in marriage
Indiscriminate spending
Lack of enthusiasm
Intolerance
Inability to cooperate with others
Egotism and vanity
Guessing instead of thinking

He also listed eight definite causes of persistence that lead to success and happiness:

Definiteness of purpose
Desire
Self-reliance
Definiteness of plans
Accurate knowledge
Cooperation
Willpower
Habit

Notice that desire, purpose, and plans are all

given. Men who are successful are men who have set goals and laid plans to reach them. It is hard to separate success from happiness.

Seeking Biblical Success

No man can truly be successful and happy unless he has a proper relationship to Jesus Christ as Lord and Savior. Even if we became president of the world's largest corporation or king of our own empire, if we were to die without accepting Christ as our Savior, we would die a failure.

What does the Bible say about success? In a manner of speaking, the Bible talks about the same things we have been discussing. Too many young adults seem to feel that religion has nothing to offer them, that it is irrelevant. Nothing is farther from the Truth. Our Lord is not just a "Sunday Blesser"; He is interested in every activity we set our hands to. He is concerned about and wants to bless our activities at school, on the job, at home, during recreation, etc.

Proverbs 23:7 says, "For as . . . [a man] thinketh in his heart, so is he." Certainly these words could have a lot of different possible meanings; but as is backed up by other verses we shall look at later, they also deal with success.

How do you think? Do you think positively? in a successful vein? Or, do you see yourself defeated and unsuccessful? Since you are what you think, you need to get your thinking straightened out. See yourself, with God's blessings on your life, accomplishing your goals. Think positively. You are

God's child, a joint or equal heir with Jesus Christ
—not just spiritually, but in every area of your
life.

Jesus said in John 16:23, 24, "And in that day
ye shall ask me nothing. Verily, verily, I say unto
you, Whatsoever ye shall ask the Father in my
name, he will give it you. Hitherto have ye asked
nothing in my name: ask, and ye shall receive,
that your joy may be full."

Jesus does not limit this prayer to certain things.
"Ask," He says, "in any area of your life. Commit
your job to God and let Him bless it. Commit your
schooling to God and let God help you."

Why does God want to do it? Jesus told us in
this verse. God wants us to be full of joy. He
knows that when we are succeeding and growing
and advancing, we are happy—not just spiritually,
but in every area of life. Commit all areas of your
life to Him to bless you. Set your goals and plans,
saturated with prayer, and move forward expect-
ing Him to bless you.

Jesus also said in John 14:12-14:

> *Verily, verily, I say unto you, He that
> believeth on me, the works that I do shall he
> do also; and greater works than these shall he
> do; because I go unto my Father. And whatso-
> ever ye shall ask in my name, that will I do,
> that the Father may be glorified in the Son.
> If ye shall ask any thing in my name, I will
> do it.*

Then, why do we not feel His presence in all

areas of our life? Because most of us expect God to handle just the spiritual, while we try to take care of the rest ourselves. But He wants all of us, and we are losers if we hold back any part.

What, then, is the answer to success? Firmly plant yourself in the hands of God. Then, with His anointing and leading, march into all areas of your life. Possess a positive outlook. Expect God to bless. Don't confess doubt, defeat, and failure. But rather, confess His presence, anointing, blessing, and victory.

The words found in Proverbs 4:20-22 are appropriate here: "My son, attend to my words; incline thine ear unto my sayings. Let them not depart from thine eyes; keep them in the midst of thine heart. For they are life unto those that find them, and health to all their flesh." We are urged to pay attention to God's Word. We are not to let it depart from our eyes, but we are to hide it in our heart.

Then, at the beginning of the sixth chapter, verse 2, the writer says "Thou art snared with the words of thy mouth, thou art taken with the words of thy mouth." Our words will lead us to victory or will send us down in defeat. One of the greatest elements of success and happiness is proper attitude—our thinking. Remember: God is interested in all of our life.

> *And I say unto you, Ask, and it shall be given you; seek, and ye shall find; knock, and it shall be opened unto you. For every one that asketh receiveth; and he that seeketh find-*

eth; and to him that knocketh it shall be opened. If a son shall ask bread of any of you that is a father, will he give him a stone? or if he ask a fish, will he for a fish give him a serpent? Or if he shall ask an egg, will he offer him a scorpion? If ye then, being evil, know how to give good gifts unto your children: how much more shall your heavenly Father give the Holy Spirit to them that ask him? (Luke 11:9-13).

Setting Goals

Goals should be set in every area of life, even the spiritual. Some people, who are sitting on church pews, are no closer to the Lord today than they were twenty years ago. Why? Because they stopped striving for a closer walk. They received a blessing and became satisfied. They set no new heights; they have no new goals to strive for.

The most important goals we can ever set are spiritual goals. The Word of God says, "But seek ye first the kingdom of God, and his righteousness; and all these things shall be added unto you" (Matthew 6:33). Our primary goals should be to strive for Christlikeness, to draw closer to God, to become more yielded vessels, and to be more open to His leading. But let us not stop here; let us set goals in other areas of life as well.

What do you personally want to accomplish in business? Set goals dealing with where you want to go and how you intend to get there. Pray much and depend upon the Lord.

Set goals for your family. What do you want to see in your marriage and family in the future? During a time when so many things are pulling against the family, the Christian family should certainly be pulling and working toward goals that will strengthen and help them attain things they desire.

Goal-setting is not easy. It takes thought and planning. Below are some suggestions:

1. Pray before thinking about or writing down goals. Seek God's leading.

2. Include in the setting of goals others to be affected; for example, family goals should be discussed by the family.

3. Set goals that are realistic and reachable. Use wisdom.

4. Be sure your goals are in line with God's Word.

5. Decide on goals that are both short-term (one to two years) and long-term (three to five years).

Remember: success is knowing where you are going and getting there.

Reaching Your Goals

Lewis Mumford once said, "A halfway leap will prove as fatal as no leap at all." Once you have decided on the goals for your life, then begin deciding how you are going to reach them. Following are some suggestions:

1. Pray daily for God's wisdom and leadership.

2. Write down your goals on paper and keep them in a handy place.

3. Daily look at your goals and write down ways to reach them.

4. Begin instigating your plans for reaching your goals. Goals on paper are worthless if no action is taken to reach them.

5. Begin to visualize yourself, by faith, with your goals reached.

6. Think, talk, and act positively!

7. Do all for the glory and praise of the Lord.

Paul's words to the Colossians seem fitting here: "And whatsoever ye do in word or deed, do all in the name of the Lord Jesus, giving thanks to God and the Father by him" (Colossians 3:17).

4

CAREER AND EDUCATION

Deciding on an education and a career is one of the most important decisions of life. It is a real challenge to choose, under God's leading, that area of work that we will spend our life doing.

Not too many years ago, a person chose his career early and stayed with it until he retired—most likely never leaving the town in which he was reared. Today, however, it is not unusual for a person to change careers two or three times and move from coast to coast during his working years.

The increased mobility of today's society can cause problems, but it also offers a tremendous challenge and opportunity for the young adult. His opportunities are unlimited. Therefore, he must make his decisions carefully and wisely, beginning with the preparation, education, and training for his chosen work.

The Learning Years

Learning does not take place just in schools. Learning is a part of life's continuing experiences. Paul Bergevin, in *Philosophy for Adult Education,* says:

> *Every adult regardless of age, mentality, race, sex, religion, size or shape can and must continue to learn in order to fulfill his nature as a developing, maturing being. . . . The adult who believes that having been to school when he was younger will suffice so far as learning is concerned is a social liability. Of course, schools aren't the only places people can learn. Actually the schools should teach people how to learn, using subjects as examples and vehicles of learning. Learning can take place anywhere, and one kind or another does. But the kind of learning that helps us become increasingly mature, that helps us identify our personal and corporate problems and handle them intelligently—this is one kind of learning that can improve the chances of the civilizing process being the winner.*

A sign seen in a printing firm in Dallas, Texas, says, "As long as you are green, you grow; when you think you are ripe, you begin to get rotten." Young adults must realize that education and learning are a continuing part of life. When a person stops learning, he becomes stale and liable.

The emphasis on learning is portrayed in the Word of God. Paul admonishes Timothy, "Study to shew thyself approved unto God, a workman that needeth not to be ashamed, rightly dividing the word of truth" (2 Timothy 2:15).

Our learning is continual. It involves growing and learning the Word of God first, but also growing in every other area of life as well.

Jesus says in Matthew 11:29, "Take my yoke upon you, and *learn* of me."

Learning of Him should be foremost, but it should also guide us to keep growing and learning in life. Let us never stop learning. Let us make reading and study a habit of life. Someday we may well look back and discover it was the best habit we ever had.

The Fourth R—the Rat Race

Young people are schooled in the three *R's*, but little preparation is given for the fourth *R:* the rat race. Many young adults leave school to enter the work world only to find pressures and tensions for which they are unprepared. This is why it is so important for us to decide upon a vocation that is both satisfying and enjoyable. Otherwise, the tension will make us miserable! Work that has as its only satisfaction the paycheck is closer to slavery than it is to the freedom of working. Experts all seem to agree that job boredom is one of the chief occupational diseases.

Finding the right vocation and the right job is one of the greatest challenges and blessings of young adulthood. However, the desire to get ahead can sometimes make us do things that, in the long run, hinder our goals.

Elizabeth B. Hurlock, in *Developmental Psychology,* says, "Some men, however, in their zeal to get ahead, work under great physical and psychological pressure. They work long hours without adequate rest; they eat at irregular times and skip regular meals in favor of sandwiches and coffee; and they work under great nervous tension. As a result they develop high blood pressure, ulcers, and many other physical disturbances that decrease their efficiency."

This is not good. God never intended for us to kill ourselves through overwork, emotional tension, and too much emphasis on "getting ahead," at the expense of our family and God.

It is God's plan for us to live a well-rounded, healthy life. In Exodus 20:9, 10, God says, "Six days shalt thou labour, and do all thy work: But the seventh day is the sabbath of the Lord thy God: in it thou shalt not do any work."

As much as God desired for us to pull aside and worship Him, He also knew that we needed at least one day a week for quiet and rest. We moderns have forgotten that lesson. We try and cram every minute with something—anything to keep us busy. Many of us are in debt, far beyond common sense, paying for recreational "toys" to fill our idle moments. We have forgotten what the word *rest* means. Consequently, the rat race gets faster, and we become more frustrated. We today have more leisure time than our forefathers ever had, yet we are killing ourselves with busyness. We must learn to rest.

Jesus knew the importance of rest. Periodically, He would turn to His weary disciples and say, "Come ye . . . apart . . . and rest a while" (Mark 6:31). He knew that occasionally we have to "come apart" to keep from "coming apart"!

A person entering his or her chosen field has the tendency to want to "do it all in a day." But the price he must pay is not worth the gain. Let us enter our work with enthusiasm, but also with concern for our health. Let us ask ourselves: "Is my life worth stretching over seventy years? or am I content for it to burn out in fifty?" Let us learn to pace ourselves and to take time to relax.

The Right Job

Being caught in the wrong job, with seemingly no way of escape, is miserable. The occupation we choose is important. We are living in the age of the half-done job. This is the day when employers are complaining about the difficulty of finding conscientious workers, when laundry men won't iron shirts, when waiters won't wait on tables, when salesmen won't sell, when students take crip courses to keep from having to work, when carpenters promise to fix broken porches "one of these days," when businessmen would rather play golf than work—leisure America!

Somewhere along the way, we have lost the concept of an honest day's work for an honest day's pay. We desperately need to find it again. Jesus says in Luke 10:7 that "the labourer is worthy of his hire." And certainly he is. But the employer is also worthy of an honest day's labor.

The young adult trying to focus his attention on a career or vocation needs to be careful of an attitude of trying to get something for nothing. The choice of a career must not be left to chance. It must not mean taking the easiest road for the moment at hand.

Many things must be considered in choosing a vocation. The young adult should ask himself, "What am I fitted for? What are my natural abilities? Where are my interests? What are my goals in life?"

There are many things to consider in choosing a career. A few are suggested here:

1. Choose a field that you are interested in. Too many young adults are frustrated in fields chosen by their parents: for example, the young man who starts a career in service because his dad and granddad were career soldiers; the young man who enters the family business because it was expected of him; the young lady who becomes a teacher because her parents felt this was a respectable job for a lady; or the young person pushed into athletics because of a parent who was never able to excel in sports. The result could very possibly be a young adult trained in his career, but totally unhappy and under

terrible emotional stress because of it.

A cartoon of several years back pictured a young man in cap and gown standing before a college auditorium with a Ph.D. degree in hand, facing his parents, saying, "Now, Dad, can I be a fireman?"

2. Choose a field within the range of your abilities.
3. Choose a field that you have the educational and financial possibilities to pursue.
4. Choose a career that offers you those things that you deem important in life.
5. Choose a career offering you fulfillment and satisfaction.
6. Choose a career that offers growth and advancement.
7. Choose a career that offers enough variety to stay interesting.
8. Choose a career that is conducive to your Christian testimony—one in which you feel you can accomplish God's will for your life.
9. Choose a career only after praying and seeking God's direction.

The Right Amount of Education

We have passed, hopefully, through the period when it was felt that everybody ought to go to college. This simply is not true. A person should obtain as much education as he is able and capable of achieving; but for many persons an education in a junior college, a trade school, or a vocational-technical high school is a far more realistic and beneficial route.

Still, college is important for the person whose chosen career requires a college degree or will benefit from a college education. Choose your college or university carefully. Select one that offers a good course of study in the area of your interest. Write for catalogs of several colleges before deciding. Do not choose your college simply because you have friends attending there. Be sure the college itself meets your requirements. If you are not sure of your definite career choice, take a liberal arts course your first year or two.

There are many junior colleges, vocational tech schools, and trade schools all over the country offering a great variety in job-skill training. Check those near you if college does not seem to fit your needs.

Wrong Choices

The difficulty in adjusting to a new occupation is evident by the statistics. Donald E. Super, in *Psychology of Careers,* points out that young adults just out of high school average eight jobs the first year, while persons in the 20-35 age bracket average five years per job, and adults over 35 average thirteen years per job. College men under 30 years of age averaged two and one-half jobs for every job held by men over 40. Because of the vast amount of job-changing, many sociologists have called the early young adult years the floundering years. This floundering may be a continuous process for some, especially in lower-level occupations.

It is common for a man to decide he is in the wrong job. When the job fits the man, it is one of life's greatest blessings; when the job fights the man, it is one of life's greatest trials. If a person finds that he is unhappy in his job, and there is nothing he can do to rectify the situation, he should change jobs or even vocations. This may be difficult if he has a family to support. But, it is still less difficult and less destructive to make a change at this point than to spend the rest of his life trying to do something his heart simply is not in.

Occupation or Calling?

God has a purpose for each person's life. The young adult choosing his vocation should remember that. God is interested in the individual through the week as well as on Sunday. God wants to use a person's job as a place of service to Him.

Elton Trueblood, in his beautiful book *Your Other Vocation* says:

> The word "vocation" has been debased in the modern world by being made synonymous with "occupation," but it is one of the gains of our time that the old word is beginning to regain its original meaning of "calling." "Behold your calling, brethren," is the old text which is now achieving new significance. On the purely secular basis the term "voca-

tion" is practically meaningless, since, unless God really is, there is no one to do the calling; but, on the Christian basis, it is a reasonable word. It still refers, in many cases, to occupation, but the conception is that each occupation can and must be conceived as a ministry.

Every man must view himself as a full-time servant of God whose primary purpose is evangelism. Trueblood goes on to say, "No amount of piety on Sunday will take the place of integrity on Wednesday. Unless we can go to work with God on Monday, we are not likely, in the long run, to have any effective worship of God on Sunday, and if we do engage in the latter, it becomes a sham!"

Our job is to share the message of Jesus Christ at the point of human contact. The way we approach our vocation is more a part of our testimony many times than what we say. Mr. Trueblood suggests that God does call persons to leave their jobs to enter full-time service; by and large, it is God's will for young adults to stay and become full-time missionaries, sharing right where they are in the work they are doing.

How do you view your job? your fellow employees? your boss? Do you view them simply as people that of necessity you must be around, or do you view them as people for whom God has a purpose?

If, Trueblood suggests, the average laymen would ever fully comprehend that he is called and in a ministry there on his job, the number of ministers would jump from one to a hundred or more and the church would undergo nothing less than a vibrant, much-needed, spiritual revolution.

The concept of a "calling" to a vocation is beginning to take root. It is not unusual to see young adults dedicate themselves to be consecrated, God-centered doctors, lawyers, laborers, and homemakers, right alongside those setting themselves aside for their "calling" to the pastorate or Christian education.

The Church's Role

Church libraries should be well stocked with books that will aid young adults in their career choice. These books should be publicized so that people know they are there. Pastors and other church staff members should read in this area and counsel as much as possible with young adults facing career choices. A professional in this area could be called upon to address young adult and youth groups and to answer questions and give guidelines.

Young adult gatherings could periodically discuss the frustrations and tensions of working and settling in a career. This interaction could be of invaluable help to those facing these pressures.

Most of all, the church can simply have the attitude "we care about what you're facing and want to help."

5

CHOOSING A MATE

A young adult faces no greater excitement nor no greater challenge than choosing a mate. Marriage is not a game. It is two people of the opposite sex making a total commitment for life. It is, therefore, worthy of a great deal of preparation, planning, and prayer. A man or woman may spend years preparing for a vocation. Marriage, however, seems to be one rare area of life where no preparation is considered necessary. Certainly, the divorce statistics show the fallacy of this feeling.

A Look at Sex Roles

Because of the many pressures facing the young adult—job, schooling, social pressures, and all the rest—what should be one of life's most beautiful experiences, in fact, becomes one of life's worst.

Society has somewhat set the pattern for the sexes. Young people are expected to align and conform to these traditional sex roles. Before they ever reach young adulthood, boys and girls are well aware of what these roles are. But, as Elizabeth B. Hurlock says in her book *Developmental Psychology,* knowing the required sex roles does not necessarily mean acceptance.

Most girls want to be wives and mothers, but not all of them want marriage and motherhood in the traditional sense. They want to train their husbands to accept more of an equalitarian role, especially if the wife works. Many young ladies today are being forced to choose between family and career or to balance the two.

The area of sex roles can be a real problem of adjustment. When two individuals come into marriage with differing concepts of the sex roles of husband and wife, there can be severe or even critical family problems. These problems will result in an uneasy and uncertain time of trying to align the varying ideas together.

This time of adjustment is less of a problem in cultures where the sex roles are rigidly fixed. In Oriental cultures, for example, the sex roles are rigidly prescribed. These roles are simply accepted and conformed to by the individuals. The same thing could be said for the early Puritans, as well. Their sex roles were based on strong religious precepts; and people, knowing what was expected of them, simply filled the roles.

However, American culture today has changed.

The roles are becoming very flexible, and this is causing much confusion in the minds of young adults. As a result, they are experiencing inner turmoil and conflict. They are asking themselves such questions as, "Do I conform to society's norm? Or, do I do what I feel is best, even though it contradicts the traditional sex role?"

Sex roles need to be clarified. Much of the problem young adults have in adjusting to marriage stems from the fact that they have not seen good sex roles (of husband and wife) modeled before them. The concern of the hour is that men will be biblical husbands and that women will be biblical wives. When this is achieved, perhaps once again we could have a return to scriptural sex roles.

A person must have a good concept of his sex role. He must know what is expected of him and be willing to conform and fit into that pattern. Why do so many fail at this task? Louis Binstock, author of *The Power of Maturity,* quotes a leading divorce lawyer as saying, "The chief basic cause of a divorce—not the trimmings—is that one or the other partner of the marriage has not learned to live with himself." We fail with others because we fail with ourselves.

Two persons come into marriage with expectations and desires that they expect to see fulfilled in their marriage relationship. Often, these expectations differ greatly between the two people because of their diverse backgrounds. What they have seen in their parents' home has greatly influenced what they expect of their own marriage relationship.

Frustration comes when the actual relationship differs from the premarital expectations.

A Look Inside Marriage

Someone once said, "Marriages are made in heaven." To this, someone quickly retorted, "So is thunder and lightning!"

Unfortunately, many marriages contain a great amount of storm and stress. A marriage does not become complete when two persons say "I do." On the contrary, it takes years to make a marriage. It takes a constant, continual effort by both members to create an intimate, meaningful, lasting family relationship.

Andre Maurois, in his book *Art of Living,* says, "Marriage is not something that can be accomplished all at once; it has to be constantly reaccomplished. A couple must never indulge in idle tranquility with the remark: 'the game is won; let's relax.' The game is never won. . . . A successful marriage is an edifice that must be rebuilt every day."

Young persons are encouraged to spend years educating themselves for a vocation and other things in life. Marriage, however, which is supposed to last for a lifetime, is entered into with little or no preparation.

Dr. Kenneth O. Gangel, writing in *The Family First,* reminds us that "happy homes take work and there is a constant danger of stagnancy in the love relationship between husband and wife. Some young people with the gleam of romance in their eyes think that if they get in contact with the right person and vibrations rise, all will be well till the end of time. Such immaturity only demonstrates a fearsome lack of readiness for marriage. Marital love requires nurture and care to not only survive, but grow to be more beautiful 20 or 30 years later than it was on the wedding day."

There are many adjustments to be made in marriage. It is rare to find a husband and wife who harbor the same ideas, who have cultivated the same sleeping habits, who both like to read in bed, who prefer the same number of blankets, who share the same hobbies, who eat the same dishes, etc.

Marriage is a life-binding contract before God. Two people before God commit themselves to one another for life. It is no longer a time of searching to find someone to please; it is from now on a life of pleasing the one you have chosen, loving him, and being loved in return. Marriage takes more than love to be successful. It requires willpower, patience, and acceptance.

Many divorces are the result of improper preparation for marriage. When the lofty ideals with which one entered marriage are not fulfilled, he gives up to try again and again and again—little realizing that marriage takes work, and years of it.

A Look at Marriage as God Sees It

God places a very important emphasis on marriage. Marriage is instituted in the very first book of the Bible: "It is not good that the man should be alone; I will make him an help meet for him"

(Genesis 2:18). God goes on to say in verse 24, "Therefore shall a man leave his father and his mother, and shall cleave unto his wife: and they shall be one flesh."

Man gives up his dependent relationship with his parents to assume a mature, intimate relationship with his wife. The Bible gives strict admonition throughout its pages concerning marriage. It tells us that marriage is the only context through which sexual relationships may take place. Premarital or extramarital relationships are an abomination in the sight of God, and those who are involved in such relationships are classified along with other sinners who will be cast into the lake of fire (Revelation 21:8).

God created marriage as a relationship whereby two mature persons could come together and unite to become one. In God's ideal marriage, one plus one equals one. Our modern society doesn't like that. Women's lib and other antibiblical trends of the day teach that one plus one equals two. God never intended it that way! His words were specific: "They shall be one flesh."

A Christian family should understand the biblical purpose of marriage. Kenneth O. Gangel, in *The Family First,* lists four purposes of a Christian marriage: fellowship, sexual fulfillment, procreation, and symbolic Truth (Ephesians 5).

In Ephesians, chapter 5, God emphasized the importance of marriage, using the marriage relationship to describe the union between Christ and the Church:

> *Husbands, love your wives, even as Christ
> also loved the church, and gave himself for it;
> That he might sanctify and cleanse it with the
> washing of water by the word, That he might
> present it to himself a glorious church, not hav-
> ing spot, or wrinkle, or any such thing; but
> that it should be holy and without blemish. So
> ought men to love their wives as their own
> bodies. He that loveth his wife loveth himself.
> . . . Nevertheless let every one of you in par-
> ticular so love his wife even as himself; and the
> wife see that she reverence her husband*
> (Ephesians 5:25-33).

Men are to love their wives as Christ loved His
bride, the Church. Men are to give themselves for
their wives as Christ gave Himself. Likewise, the
wife is to "reverence" her husband: that is, she "no-
tices him, regards him, honors him, prefers him, ven-
erates and esteems him; and that she defers to
him, praises him, and loves and admires him ex-
ceedingly" (*Amplified*). Christ takes the Church
as she is with all her faults and presents her to
God. Husbands and wives are to do the same with
one another.

The marriage relationship is an intimate one. It
takes work and a lot of sharing. A marriage cannot be built around a home situation where either
of the partners is always ready to go out the door.

A Look at Those Who Do Not Marry

Our society tends to categorize everyone over
thirty and still unmarried as having something

wrong with them. However, marriage is definitely not for everyone. It is not God's will for everyone to marry. Paul speaks of this when he writes to the Corinthians:

But to the unmarried people and to the widows, I declare that it is well—good, advantageous, expedient and wholesome—for them to remain [single] even as I do.

My desire is to have you free from all anxiety and distressing care. The unmarried [man] is anxious about the things of the Lord, how he may please the Lord; But the married man is anxious about worldly matters, how he may please his wife. And he is drawn in diverging directions—his interests are divided, and he is distracted [from his devotion to God]. And the unmarried woman or girl is concerned and anxious about the matters of the Lord, how to be wholly separated and set apart in body and spirit; but the married woman has her cares [centered] in earthly affairs, how she may please her husband (1 Corinthians 7:8, 32-34; Amplified).

Some people, Paul says, can serve God better unmarried. It is no disgrace to be unmarried. For some this is God's will, because of special callings or ministries. Marriage is a holy institution, instituted by God, but it should not be entered into just because it is the thing to do.

A Look at Preparation for Marriage

Marriage is for keeps. It is a permanent relationship.

Wherefore they are no more twain, but one flesh. What therefore God hath joined together, let not man put asunder (Matthew 19:6).

For the woman which hath an husband is bound by the law to her husband so long as he liveth; but if the husband be dead, she is loosed from the law of her husband. So then if, while her husband liveth, she be married to another man, she shall be called an adulteress: but if her husband be dead, she is free from that law; so that she is no adulteress, though she be married to another man (Romans 7:2, 3).

Realizing that God draws two people together until parted by death, the couple should not enter into this intimate relationship until they have made preparations. Persons entering marriage need to realize that there will be differences. Two people from different backgrounds and different life-styles will naturally have different ideas on what they want out of marriage. Marriage is not some utopia where both parties are always happy. Rather, it is a relationship of two very human individuals who at times are unhappy or discouraged. But Christians realize that their marriage relationship is for keeps; and when these times of stress come, they work through them.

H. Norman Wright, in *Ways to Help Them Learn (Adult)*, says, "Before the ceremony a young adult should seriously analyze his motivation for getting married. Why marriage? Why this person?

What do I expect to get and give to the marriage relationship? Many have not asked this question nor have their churches assisted them in this regard."

Know why you are getting married. Settle in your mind what you feel you can expect from your mate and what your mate can expect from you. Pondering these expectations, discuss them, and come to an agreement about them with your prospective spouse before the ceremony.

A Look at How Mates Are Chosen

Choosing a mate can be a very traumatic experience. First of all, the young adult is inexperienced in this area; and second, he is most often swayed by his present feelings rather than by his judgment and logic. However, no decision in life is worth any more prayer and honest good sense than the choice of the person with whom you will spend the remainder of your life.

A person would be a fool to enter a business partnership with one he does not know. If he did and lost his shirt, his friends would most likely say it served him right for not being more careful and cautious.

So, also it should be in marriage. Why are there so many divorces? There is not enough time spent in preparation for marriage. Young couples do not take the time to really get to know one another before marriage. Christian young couples do not spend enough time in prayer before making this very important decision.

Louis Binstock, in *The Power of Maturity,* lists

statistics on divorce put out by the Institute of Life
Insurance. He states that 26.5 percent of all divorces take place in the first two years of marriage,
and that 51.3 percent take place in the first five
years of marriage. The Institute of Life Insurance
concludes that the younger the bride, the greater the
chance that the marriage will fail. When both bride
and groom are in their teens, the chances that the
marriage will fail are twice as great as they are
when the bride is at least twenty-one and the groom
is over twenty-four.

Several things should be considered in choosing
a mate. Age is an important factor. It seems it is
best for the man to be a couple of years older than
the woman. Both partners should be in good health.
It is generally best for both partners to have ap-
proximately equal levels of abilities and education.
A Christian should marry someone else in the faith.
How often tragedy could have been avoided, had this
advice been heeded! A marriage without Christ as
the foundation has two strikes against it before it
begins. If only one member is a Christian, there
still is no excuse for not taking the needs and problems of the young marriage to God for direction.

A Look at Maturity in Marriage

Persons entering marriage must realize that they
are no longer two persons, but one. In this relationship, there is no room for selfishness. The *I* must be
dropped in favor of *we, us,* and *ours.* This sometimes becomes a real source of contention.

Someone has said there are three parts of courtship: wooing, winning, and welding. Unfortunately, we spend months and even years on the first two areas of wooing and winning, but very little time on the equally important task of welding. This involves doing those things that weld two persons closer together as a couple.

Howard and Jeanne Hendricks, writing in *Adult Education in the Church,* edited by Roy B. Zuck and Gene A. Getz, put it this way: "Most families reach whatever degree of cohesion they achieve as matter of chance. If husbands and wives gave only one-tenth as much time to discussing and planning the future of their relationship as they do their business or even their social life, their marriages would grow in meaning and cohesion. Many couples spend more time keeping their automobiles clean than in keeping their romance shining." It takes work to keep a healthy, maturing marriage. It does not come overnight.

A successful marriage is not one where Prince Charming and Lady Lovely, two perfectly matched young adults with the same interests, backgrounds, and aspirations come together to form a beautiful marriage. Rather, a successful marriage is one where two people of perhaps unmatched backgrounds, interests, hobbies, educations, and the like come together in marriage; and until death separates them, they work together to communicate and to solve all the problems and differences of opinions that constantly arise. Naturally, this does not come overnight. It takes time to be married—time to communicate, time to listen to one another. Unfortu-

nately, in the average home, its members spend the
night in the same house, but the rest of the time
are gone or are in the process of leaving to go somewhere else for some "very important" activity. They
then wonder why the family relationship is strained
and things are not working well. Families must
take time to be together—to enjoy the love and fellowship of family togetherness.

Many marriages end in divorce before they are
given a chance. Dreams are unrealized; things do
not work out as hoped; so the persons divorce and
go on in search of the dream again—only, most
likely, to see it end again in failure. Young adults
need to enter marriage realizing that there will be
differences, but determining to work them out. Marriage takes time. A couple must work at it constantly
and continually. It certainly is one of the exciting
challenges of young adulthood.

6

BECOMING A BIBLICAL HUSBAND

We live in a confused world. The roles of husband and wife are being intermingled and, most often, totally ignored. What about the man who wants to be all that God wants him to be? Does the Bible offer any assistance? Definitely so! The Bible gives some very definite guidelines; unfortunately they are generally overlooked and not practiced.

Writing in the April, 1974, issue of *New Wine,* Derek Prince says, "In our society the wife is often referred to as the 'homemaker.' However, this is true only in a secondary sense. In the economy of God, the man is primarily the homemaker—because he will make it whatever it is to become. The father is the key to the establishment of the home. It is upon his shoulders that God has placed the responsibility and the authority to establish a home that will fulfill the design of a loving heavenly Father. When the man takes his rightful position, then the woman takes hers beside him as helpmeet."

Men, God has given us charge of our family. It makes no difference if we win the world for Christ, for if we lose our family, in God's sight we are a failure.

In *Art of Living,* Andre Maurois quotes Balzac as saying, "Many young husbands are so ignorant of women that they make him think of orangutans trying to play the violin." Whether this be true or not is speculation, but from observation, it does seem true that the average husband and father knows absolutely nothing about his God-ordained role in the family.

Heavenly Homes

> *Therefore shall ye lay up these my words in your heart and in your soul, and bind them for a sign upon your hand, that they may be as frontlets between your eyes. And ye shall teach them your children, speaking of them when thou sittest in thine house, and when thou walkest by the way, when thou liest down, and when thou risest up. And thou shalt write them upon the door posts of thine house, and upon thy gates: That your days may be multiplied, and the days of your children, in the land which the Lord sware unto your fathers to give them, as the days of heaven upon the earth* (Deuteronomy 11:18-21).

The expression "heaven on earth" is used many times as an everyday cliche. Few people realize it comes from the Bible; fewer still realize that it is given in reference to the home. How many Christian homes today could be described as "heaven on earth"? Many, unfortunately, could best be described by the other extreme. Yet, this is God's plan: that the home so manifest God's presence and God's love that it is a representation of the nature of heaven right here on earth.

Elton Trueblood, in his excellent book *Your Other Vocation,* very aptly describes the problem:

The shame of many a supposed home today is that it is largely a place where people sleep part of the night, but not really a scene of uniting experiences of all members, older and younger. Common meals become more and more infrequent while unhurried family conferences are out of the question. It is futile to talk to people about grace at meals if they do not even have the meals.

The average home is simply a place where family members pass one another in the halls on their way out. A picture of heaven? Hardly! We cannot get out of our responsibility to fulfill our God-called roles in the home. Even if one parent refuses to fulfill his role, that does not relieve the other parent, before God, of fulfilling his role in the family. Each parent stands before God responsible for his role whether or not his marriage partner is fulfilling his role. As Derek Prince says in the aforementioned article, "If our religion does not work at home, it does not work—period."

In Part II of his article in the May, 1974, issue of *New Wine,* Mr. Prince states:

The tragic disaster of the American home is the renegade male. Some of you men may feel that the word "renegade" is too strong—almost insulting. However, I use it advisedly. A "renegade" is one who "reneges," and the vast majority of American males have reneged from the three primary responsibilities—as husbands, fathers, and spiritual leaders. It has left us with a matriarchal society, dominated by women.

Let me ask you this: who—if anybody— normally prays with the children at night? Who gets them ready for Sunday school? Who reads them Bible stories? Who prays when the child is sick? In the majority of cases, it is the mother. The mother should indeed share in the spiritual growth of the child; but it is the father who is called upon by God to be the initiator and leader in the spiritual life of the family.

The crying need of the day is heavenly homes. To get them, we must have men willing to be God's men, filling their God-ordained role.

Loving Husbands

In Colossians 3:19 Paul admonishes, "Husbands, love your wives, and be not bitter against them." In 1 Corinthians 11:3 he states, "But I would have you know, that the head of every man is Christ; and the head of the woman is the man; and the head of Christ is God."

Headship is a part of being a husband. It has always been so. Eternally, the Father is the head over Christ, and this relationship is carried over into the marriage relationship. But it is not a dictatorial relationship; it is a relationship of love.

Dr. Kenneth O. Gangel, in *The Family First,* gives a list published by the League of Large Families headquartered in Brussels, Belgium. The list contains the seven most frequently chosen failings of husbands obtained from a survey of wives. They were lack of tenderness, lack of politeness, lack of sociability, failure to understand the wife's temperament and peculiarities, unfairness in financial matters, frequency of snide remarks· and sneers at the wife in company or before the children, and lack of plain honesty and truthfulness. This was a secular survey; but, as Dr. Gangel points out, it is amazing how many of these points of complaint would be removed if the husband were acting in line with his biblical role.

One of the basic complaints against husbands is that they do not listen. Listening is not one-sided. For communication to take place in the family, both parties must learn to be good listeners. Everyone wants to be heard, because in being heard he gains the feeling of being known. Inattentiveness conveys to the other party disinterest. Disinterest portrays lack of love. Of course, this is not only the husband's fault. The wife who chatters endlessly has a tendency to teach her husband how to tune her out. On the other hand, the husband needs to realize that women, in general, feel the need to talk about simple things—little things that they have faced through the day.

Reuel L. Howe, in *Creative Years*, says about listening:

Listening as an act of love is a two-sided responsibility, one belonging to the speaker in which she invites listening with worthwhile meaning, and the other responsibility belonging to the listener who seeks to give his whole attention to the person through what is being said. The speaker loves the hearer with the meaning she is trying to convey, and the listener loves the speaker with his single-hearted concentrated attention to her in the moment of communication. When the wife has been heard, and therefore loved (or it may be the husband who has been heard and loved), she may now express her love by listening to her husband, and he by speaking meaningfully to her. He who listens loves, and he who speaks loves. And love gives each the grace to reverse roles by becoming speaker instead of listener, and listener instead of speaker.

Only when a man and woman are really present to each other in this way is a love relationship possible, and love is the power that enables people to be really present to each other. And certainly marriage without this Mutual presentness and versatility is an impossibility.

Dr. Kenneth O. Gangel, in *The Family First,* lists five things that characterize a biblical husband.

First, a biblical husband is a lover.

Husbands, love your wives, even as Christ also loved the church, and gave himself for it;

So ought men to love their wives as their own bodies. He that loveth his wife loveth himself.

Nevertheless let every one of you in particular so love his wife even as himself; and the wife see that she reverence her husband (Ephesians 5:25, 28, 33).

This is not just love in a natural, desire-oriented sense, but the word *love* is from the Greek word *agapao,* which is the same word used in John 3:16. Men should love their wives in the same all-comprehensive way that Christ loves His Church. This is also brought out in 1 Peter 3:7: "Likewise, ye husbands, dwell with them according to knowledge, giving honour unto the wife, as unto the weaker vessel, and as being heirs together of the grace of life; that your prayers be not hindered."

Second, a biblical husband is a provider and protector. In 1 Timothy 5:8, Paul admonishes young Timothy, "But if any provide not for his own, and specially for those of his own house, he hath denied the faith, and is worse than an infidel." A man is responsible for the support of his family. He should see that its members are cared for without putting pressure on the wife to work so they can have more "things."

Third, a biblical husband is a teacher. In

Deuteronomy, chapters 6, 11, and 31, the Word stresses nurture as a main role of the home. Paul, writing to the Corinthians in 1 Corinthians 14:35, tells the wife to ask questions of her husband at home. Again, this stresses the role of the husband as the spiritual teacher of the home. Unfortunately, most husbands delegate this teaching duty to the wives by default.

Fourth, the biblical husband is a ruler. First Peter 3:6 says, "Even as Sara obeyed Abraham, calling him lord: whose daughters ye are, as long as ye do well, and are not afraid with any amazement." The husband is the head of the home. But he can function as the head only as the wife puts him there and allows him to function in his God-called role. God's plan is Jesus Christ in subjection to the Father; the husband in subjection to Jesus Christ; and the wife in subjection to the husband.

Fifth, the biblical husband is priest of his family. Really he is prophet and priest. As prophet he comes to his family with God's Word. As priest he has the responsibility of taking his family to God.

God has an ordained role for every husband and father to fill. Few men completely fill that role.

Biblical Fathers

Much is said and implied in the Bible about fatherhood. In Ephesians 3:14, 15, Paul says: "For this cause I bow my knees unto the Father of our Lord Jesus Christ, Of whom the whole family in heaven and earth is named." (The King James Version says *family* here, but the Greek word is *patria,* from *pater* or "father." J. B. Phillips translates it "fatherhood," which is a more accurate rendering of the Greek.) Paul is saying that God is the Father of Jesus Christ, and that this relationship becomes the pattern for the office of a father on earth. All earthly fatherhood, then, becomes a projection of the Fatherhood of God. He is our example.

Derek Prince, in his two-part series on "Fatherhood" in *New Wine,* April and May, 1974, states that a father has two obligations toward his children: communication and education, in that order. The channels of communication must be open before education can take place. The father's giving instruction is not enough; the child must also be willing to receive it.

As we have pointed out before, Christ has the offices that have been delegated to Him by the Father. Those offices are prophet, priest, and king (or governor). Every father stands before his family in this role patterned by Jesus Christ in His relationship to His Father and to His Church. Every father must be the prophet, priest, and governor of his home, or that home will fail to fulfill its role as an example of the Church in miniature.

The Old Testament also supports the New Testament teaching on this subject, referred to earlier in Deuteronomy 11:18-21. Here parents are given an outline of their responsibility before God, with the father taking the leading role in teaching God's words and His ways to his children.

Unfortunately, most parents have delegated this

responsibility to the church. God never intended for the church to be the main religious educator of the children; the family has this responsibility. The church is to support the family. A look at any modern family that delegates its religious education to the church is example enough that this will not work. Fathers must fill their roles as religious educators.

The fact that the father is to take the lead is evidenced by such scriptures as Ephesians 6:4 ("And, ye fathers, provoke not your children to wrath: but bring them up in the nurture and admonition of the Lord") and Colossians 3:21 ("Fathers, provoke not your children to anger, lest they be discouraged"). Mothers certainly are involved, but God has given the leadership role to fathers.

Spiritual Leaders

Derek Prince, in the aforementioned article says, "Unless the father takes his place, accepts his responsibilities, and stands as God intends him to stand as the head of his house, God's program for the home cannot work. If the father will not provide proper headship in the home, the home will fall into disorder."

Paul, writing to the Ephesians, says, "Awake thou that sleepest, and arise from the dead, and Christ shall give thee light" (Ephesians 5:14). There is no intention to take this verse out of context, but this is exactly what is needed by most fathers today. They are asleep and dead to their responsibilities. They need to allow Christ to illuminate them and to make them what they should be.

One requirement of a leader in the church, Paul says, is that he rule his own house well (1 Timothy 3:4). The word *rule* denotes "the exercising of governmental authority." The standard is that if a man cannot control his own home, he is in no way qualified to rule the church of God. The home, therefore, is a testing ground. Failure at home—no matter how successful a man may be in other areas —means abject failure in God's sight.

Ultimately, each father and husband must ask himself the questions: "How do I rate as a husband? as a father? Am I fulfilling my God-called role? Disregarding all other areas of my life, am I successful at home?" If you fail there, my friend, before God you are a failure.

The call of the hour is for men with courage— spiritual courage to stand and become all that God wants and expects them to be. The ranks are slim. Have you that much courage?

7

BECOMING A BIBLICAL WIFE

They say a wife and husband, bit by bit,
Can rear between themselves a mighty wall,
So thick they cannot speak with ease through
   it,
Nor can they see across it, it stands so tall.
Its nearness frightens them, but each alone
Is powerless to tear its bulk away; and each
Dejected wishes he had known
For such a wall, some magic thing to say.
So let us build with master art, my dear,
A bridge of love between your life and mine,
A bridge of tenderness and very near,
A bridge of understanding, strong and fine,
Till we have formed so many lovely ties,
There never will be room for walls to rise.

                                        Anonymous

Just as God has a biblical role for the husband to fill, so He has one for the wife. God is specific in His Word about marriage relationships. The current women's liberation movement is probably one of the most antibiblical movements the world has ever seen. The current cigarette ad reminds us, "You've come a long way, baby!"—but, it doesn't say which way. The modern movement calls for no set roles in society; instead, it advocates unisex. The movement is effecting dress—both in society at large and in the home.

Commenting on this, Dr. Kenneth O. Gangel says in *The Family First:*

> *The ridiculous performance of the contemporary Woman's Liberation Movement is a demonstrable example of what excesses can be reached when human beings reject God's distinctive place for them in the scheme of home and society. Even in Christian homes today one of the biggest pitfalls on the path to happy family living is the distortion of Biblical roles for family members.*

Women who want to be women, in the fullest sense of their holy calling, must be women willing to go against the current trend of society, to stand for Christian values, and to fill the role Scripture has set for them.

The Biblical Pattern for the Wife

The wife does have a pattern to follow. An example has been given her. Paul, writing to the Ephesians, says:

> *Wives, be subject—be submissive and adapt yourselves—to your own husbands as*

[*a service*] *to the Lord. For the husband is head of the wife as Christ is the Head of the church, Himself the Savior of* [*His*] *body. As the church is subject to Christ, so let wives also be subject in everything to their husbands. Husbands, love your wives, as Christ loved the church and gave Himself up for her, So that He might sanctify her, having cleansed her by the washing of water with the Word, That He might present the church to Himself in glorious splendor, without spot or wrinkle or any such things—that she might be holy and faultless. Even so husbands should love their wives as* [*being in a sense*] *their own bodies. He who loves his own wife loves himself* (Ephesians 5:22-28; *Amplified*).

Thus, we see that Christ chooses His relationship to His body the Church, to describe the relationship of a man to his wife. Jesus loves the Church. He doesn't rule her like a dictator; but He loves her, forgives her faults, and works with her as she grows. A husband is to love his wife in this same way. He is not to lord it over her, but in love he is to govern his home. The wife, likewise, is to be in submission to her husband, as the Church is in submission to the Lord Jesus Christ.

The Biblical Role of the Wife

Derek Prince, writing on "Fatherhood" in the May, 1974, issue of *New Wine,* describes the wife's relationship to her husband beautifully:

Jesus said three things about His relationship with the Father, all of which apply equally to the relationship of the wife to the husband.

First, He said, "I and my Father are one" (John 10:30). There was complete unity between Jesus and His Father. Being one with the Father, Jesus was also equal with the Father. Philippians 2:6 tells us that He had a divine right to be equal with God. He was God.

In the same manner, the husband and the wife are one. The Bible tells us they are "one flesh" (Genesis 2:4; Matthew 19:5, 6). . . . The scripture clearly indicates that God considers the husband and wife as equals in the body of Christ (Galatians 3:28).

The second thing that Jesus said about His relationship to the Father was that God requires "that all men should honour the Son, even as they honour the Father" (John 5:23) . . . The attitude of the husband to his wife should reflect that of Father to Christ. The husband should delight to honor and lift up his wife. He should do everything within his power to make her feel respected, honoured, praised and esteemed. . . .

What would happen if we men consistently treated our wives in this way? In most cases they would gladly and willingly acknowledge our headship. . . .

This brings us to the third facet of the

Father/Son relationship. Jesus also said, "The Father is greater than I" (John 14:28). Here is an apparent paradox: Jesus is equal with the Father, yet He says that the Father is greater than He. . . . He did not fight for recognition or authority, but willingly submitted Himself to His Father and allowed His Father to fill His rightful place of Headship. By remaining in submission to His Father, Jesus maintained the unity within the Godhead. Had He left His voluntary place of submission, the unity of the Godhead would have been broken.

Likewise, even though the wife is one with, and therefore also equal with, the husband, God calls on her to submit herself to her husband for the sake of the unity and order in the home. If she refuses her submission, there will be a breakdown of unity in the home, and disorder will result. This places a tremendous responsibility upon the wife. It means that no man can truly be the head of his home unless his wife yields to his authority. No head can function without a neck to hold it up; and no man can truly be the head of his home without the voluntary submission and support of his wife.

God seems to stress two things in the marriage relationship: (1) To the husband He stresses, "Love your wife." Husbands seem to take wives for granted, so God reinforces this point with added emphasis. (2) To the wife He stresses, "Submit to your husband." This is difficult for the woman, so God likewise emphasizes this point. When a husband loves his wife as he is supposed to, and when the wife submits to her husband's headship as she is told to, the marriage conforms to the pattern set by the relationship of the Father and the Son, and Christ and the Church.

Kenneth O. Gangel, in *The Family First,* lists five roles of the biblical wife: she is encouraging in her relationship to her husband; she is loving; she is submissive; she is consistent and stable; and she is attractive.

First, she is encouraging. Gangel quotes Dr. Popenoe as saying, "To a man, one of the main advantages of a home, is that it offers him a refuge from the troubles of the day. Life in the modern business or industrial world is not a picnic. He is fighting all day long, in one sense or another. When the whistle blows, he longs for peace, harmony, comfort, love. . . . The wife who creates that atmosphere in the home, who fills that place in her husband's life, knows her business."

Second, she is loving. In Ephesians 5, Paul calls it "reverence." The wife is not reminded to love as much as the husband is, perhaps because a woman can love more consistently, without her attention being diverted by business, etc.

Third, she is submissive. Paul deals with this in Ephesians 5:22-24 and again in Colossians 3:18. Peter mentions it in 1 Peter 3:1. In Ephesians Paul says that a wife is to be submissive to her husband "as unto the Lord." In Colossians he says that she is to be submissive "as it is fit in the Lord." And Peter says that unsaved husbands will be won by a wife's godly submission. So a woman is not just to be in submission to a husband who is a Christian, but to an unsaved husband as well.

Fourth, she is consistent and stable. The wife tends to be the stabilizing factor in the home. She needs to be very stable. In her role of wife and mother she must go about her tasks and fulfill her roles in such a way as to make the home a steady, peaceful shelter in a tumultuous world.

Finally, she is attractive. Someone once said, "Some women are failures as wives because they are first failures as women." Too many marriages have failed because once the ceremony was completed, the wife no longer sensed a need to stay attractive and neat. A woman should keep herself looking, acting, and smelling feminine. She must be not only a wife, but also her husband's lover and closest friend.

The Biblical Authority in the Home

It has already been mentioned, but deserves repeating: God has a definite chain of authority. The husband/wife relationship is very important as a parallel of Christ's relationship to the Church. Paul, in 1 Corinthians 11:3, gives us God's chain of command: "But I would have you know, that the head of every man is Christ; and the head of the woman is the man; and the head of Christ is God." This chain of authority originates in the Godhead and is then carried over into the home. Paul says the Father has authority over the Son, Jesus Christ. Christ is the Head; and, therefore, He is in authority over the man. The man similarly, is the head of his wife.

There is no dictative relationship between the Father and the Son; it is an authoritative relationship based on love. The same is true of the union between the Lord and the husband, and the husband and his wife. Love is the basis of the authority. One governs in love, while the other submits in love. All authority extends back to the heavenly Father. Christ has authority because He is in submission to the Father. The husband has authority because he submits to Christ. The wife has authority as she submits to her husband.

The Biblical Plan for Forgiveness

Forgiveness is one of the crying needs of the day in which we live. It is needed in all areas of life. Nowhere, though, is it needed more than in the home. People seem to have a hard time forgiving. Again, this is contingent on love.

Paul, in 1 Corinthians 13, deals with love in a beautiful way:

> *Love endures long and is kind; love is not jealous; love is not out for display; it is not conceited or unmannerly; it is neither self-seeking nor irritable, nor does it take account of a suffered wrong. It takes no pleasure in injustice, but it sides happily with truth. It covers up everything, has unquenchable faith,*

hopes under all circumstances, endures without limit (1 Corinthians 13:4-7; *Berkeley*).

Love knows how to forgive.

Jesus says in Mark 11:25, 26 that we are to forgive so that we may be forgiven! No one wants the Lord to remember his wrongs and failures like he remembers the wrongs and failures of his peers. God says that when He forgives us, our wrongs are placed in the sea of His forgetfulness, to be remembered no more (see Psalm 103:12; Jeremiah 31:34). That should be the pattern of our forgiveness of others. When we are wronged, let us forgive and forget; for unforgiveness has a tragic result: unanswered prayer (Mark 11:25, 26).

Reuel L. Howe, in *Creative Years,* says, "Another occasion on which love as responsibility may show itself is when a relationship is endangered by the offense of one of its partners. When this happens, one of two responses is possible. Either the one partner may point an accusing finger and thus place full blame on the 'guilty' one, or, out of love, he may seek to determine what part he may have played in causing the other to offend."

Paul deals with forgiveness in Galatians 6:1, 2: "Brethren, if a man be overtaken in a fault, ye which are spiritual, restore such an one in the spirit of meekness; considering thyself, lest thou also be tempted. Bear ye one another's burdens, and so fulfil the law of Christ."

Forgiveness is badly needed in the marriage relationship. Love knows how to forgive.

8

REARING CHILDREN

One of the most challenging and important roles of young adults is rearing children. Nothing in life is any more important than the children God has placed in our home. They are to be reared for Him and in knowledge of Him. This involves a great deal of discipline and correction thoroughly saturated with a spirit of love. Someone has said that everything in the modern home is run by switches except the kids. In all too many homes, even Christian homes, this is true: "switches" aren't used to turn kids on.

God puts the child into the home to be molded and reared according to God's Word. Earl F. Zeigler, in his book *Christian Education of Adults,* says, "The primary factor in molding the child is neither the church nor the school, but the home. Therefore, it seems truer to say that the young adults are the hope of the world. They are in transition and therefore quite teachable; but even more important, they have or soon will have the young in their homes."

Unfortunately, we are witnessing the decay of the family. Few families are the close-knit units that they once were. Today's family does little more together than share an occasional meal. Bill Vaughn's caricature of the American family is one describing everyone sitting silently in front of his own TV, eating his own TV dinner, and waiting for his own telephone to ring. This is a far cry from God's purpose for the home and family!

Dr. Kenneth O. Gangel, addressing himself to this subject in *The Family First*, says, "There is no question about the Biblical position on the primacy of the family. Long before God called into existence schools and churches, He designed the basic unit of society in the garden of Eden. There is no evidence in scripture that this emphasis has ever changed."

The family today is delegating to other institutions—like the school and the church—functions and responsibilities that God gave to the home. Many things influence a child: family, school, neighborhood, associates, etc. But none should have any more effect on him or change him more than the family unit when it is functioning in its God-called role.

Submission

Children, obey your parents in the Lord: for this is right. Honour thy father and mother; which is the first commandment

*with promise; That it may be well with thee,
and thou mayest live long on the earth. And,
ye fathers, provoke not your children to
wrath: but bring them up in the nurture and
admonition of the Lord* (Ephesians 6:1-4).

Paul, in writing to the Ephesians, speaks of the
family relationships. No matter what the age of a
child is—be he four or forty—he is still to honor
and reverence his parents. Paul is dealing here
with submission: Children, obey your parents, for
this is God's plan and pattern. Honor them, or as
The Amplified Bible says "esteem and value [them]
as precious."

There is a dual responsibility placed here on the
child and the parent: submission and love on the
part of children, and respect and love on the part
of parents. This is God's plan of submission: children to parents, wives to husbands, and husbands
to God. All members of the family, in a sense, put
aside their own individual desires for the sake of
the corporate good of the family unit. Through
this, Dr. Gangel says they are in submission one
to another, and collectively to the Lordship of Jesus Christ.

Fence Building

Parents are to keep their children in order. Paul,
writing to Timothy, says that a bishop is "one that
ruleth well his own house, having his children in
subjection with all gravity; (For if a man know not
how to rule his own house, how shall he take care

of the church of God?)" (1 Timothy 3:4, 5).
Paul makes it pretty plain that he considers a
man completely unfit to hold leadership positions
in the church if he does not have the ability to
lead his family. This is one qualification that has
been completely ignored by most local congrega-
tions and denominations in selecting ministers.
Paul bluntly says, "If a man can't govern his own
house, how in the world can he expect to govern
God's!"

We have a precious promise in Proverbs 22:6:
"Train up a child in the way he should go: and
when he is old, he will not depart from it." This
is our promise from God. Now, the responsibility
is on us. We must build some fences.

There is a big difference in discipline and correction. Discipline is not spanking, punishing, etc.;
discipline is building fences. Correction is what
happens when the fences are crossed.

How do we build fences? Very carefully! The
admonition has been given, "Train up a child in
the way he should go . . . and be sure you are
going that way yourself." We teach our children
in many ways, and none is any greater than the
way we live and act.

Dr. James Dobson, in his tremendous book *Dare
to Discipline,* says that discipline must be balanced
with love. He illustrates it by saying that love and
control must be equally balanced. All love and no
control results in children who are rebellious and
unprepared for mature life. All control and no
love results in tyranny where the children grow up

in resentment. Love and control must be balanced. Fences must be built, but they must be built in love, strengthened with understanding and communication.

The challenge of building fences is a tremendous challenge. Elton Trueblood, in *Your Other Vocation,* says:

> No matter how much a man may be concerned with his work in the world, he cannot normally care about it as much as he cares about his family. . . . We can change business associates, if we need to, and we can leave a poor job for a better one, but we cannot change sons. If we lose the struggle in our occupational interests, we can try again; but if we lose with our children, our loss is terribly and frighteningly final. A man who cares more for his work than he cares for his family is generally accounted abnormal or perverse and justifiably so. He is one who has not succeeded in getting his values straight; he fails to recognize what the true priorities in life are.

Fences must be built. The parents who refuse to give their children guidance in living by building fences are, in effect, saying, "I don't love you enough to help you prepare for adulthood."

Children reared without discipline are headed for a terrible time in marriage, for marriage is a very strong discipline. It is no accident that the trend the last twenty years to be very lax disciplinarians in the home has been marked by a sharp increase in divorce rates.

Also, children reared without discipline have a hard time submitting to Christ as Savior; for, again, Christianity is a very strong discipline. A child who has never been taught submission and obedience finds the life Christ offers very hard to conform to and accept, for in a very real sense he has been taught that he is his own master and that he can do his own thing and get away with it.

Erect fences carefully, not hastily. For example, Johnny is late getting home. He was told he could go to Billy's and play for an hour, and it has now been three hours. Dad is about to climb the wall. Finally, Johnny comes in.

What does Dad say? "Johnny, you'll never go over to Billy's again!"

What has happened? Dad very hurriedly, and in a rage, has built a fence. But it's a fence he does not mean to erect and one that he will pull down tomorrow. So he comes across inconsistent. Fences must be erected, but erected fairly.

A child needs fences. He should have curfews, rules, and regulations to live by and to help him mature. To give him nothing is to say, "I don't love you," and to tell God we refuse to rear our children for Him.

We must give our children room to grow. We must allow them to make minor decisions at first; then help them learn to make decisions on their own. But let us be sure the fences are up, and they know the boundaries.

Broken Fences

There are times, quite frequently, when the fence is torn down and the rules are broken. It is time for correction. This is not just saying, "Now Johnny." It is much more than this.

Proverbs 13:1 gives instruction to children: "A wise son heareth his father's instruction." But Proverbs 13:24 also tells parents what to do when the instruction is ignored: "He that spareth his rod hateth his son: but he that loveth him chasteneth him betimes."

It is God's order and will for children to obey their parents. Ephesians 6:1, 2 says, "Children, obey your parents in the Lord: for this is right. Honour thy father and mother." The promise is that if children will do this, they will enjoy long life. Colossians 3:20 says, "Children, obey your parents in all things: for this is well pleasing unto the Lord." In the very next verse fathers are encouraged not to provoke children to anger or to discourage them.

Children must be corrected, but in a spirit of love. Even if we are upset at their actions, let us be sure our love comes across.

Correction must also be consistent. If the child is punished today for something about which nothing is said tomorrow, then we haven't accomplished anything. Correction must be systematic.

Motivation

One big challenge in rearing children is motivating them to realize their potential. This does not mean we should push them to reach all the goals we have set for them; but we should encourage them in their own endeavors.

In *Philosophy for Adult Education,* Paul Bergevin says, "The parent who insists that his child be a winner at any cost or that he follow a program unsuited to the child's talent or wishes, is setting up potential emotional problems with which the child may not be able to cope successfully in later years. Being as good as you can be and being the best are quite different goals."

Many parents try to live their children's lives for them and use them to accomplish feats they did not accomplish in their own lives. Children have a right to be their best in the areas of their own interests and desires. Encouragement and love in helping our children to realize and reach realistic goals and accomplishments will lead them to a fulfilling experience and give them a better self-concept.

Louis Binstock, in his book *The Power of Maturity,* lists ten basic rules for maturity in our relationship with our children:

1. *You must know your child as he really is —and then accept him for what he is. This does not mean you overlook faults, but simply that you don't expect him to be what he isn't.*
2. *Act upon what you know about your child.*
3. *Love and care for your child.*
4. *Be honest with your child.*

5. *Guide your child.*
6. *Don't be afraid of your child.*
7. *Don't be overdemanding.*
8. *Don't expect gratitude.*
9. *Don't be overprotective.*
10. *Praise your child.*

The best thing we can do to motivate our children is to set for them a good example of a biblical mother and father. Our society has a tendency to breed in us a desire for more "things." We parents soon get snared in the materialistic trap until we are trying constantly to get more. All the while our children see nothing of what the Bible says parents should be. The family's "wants" rather than its "needs" dictate the work schedules.

No doubt there are many families in which the wife is working simply to help the family get the basic needs of life. However, in many families the motivation for maternal employment is strictly materialistic. Children need full-time parents, not baby-sitters. Fathers must provide for their families, true; but families where Mom and Dad get up, spend thirty frantic minutes getting Junior ready for the baby-sitter, and then ten hours later pick him up to feed him and get him in bed are asking for trouble.

The best thing you can do for your children, Dad and Mom, is give them your love and presence. Don't give your children to the world by default. Be God's father! Be God's mother! Train up your child in the Word! God's promise to you is that later in life, the child will not depart from that training.

"Jesus said unto him, Thou shalt love the Lord thy God with all thy heart, and with all thy soul, and with all thy mind. This is the first and great commandment. And the second is like unto it, Thou shalt love thy neighbour as thyself" (Matthew 22:37-39).

How do we teach children and motivate them to such high and worthy living, and to such standards as this? By example. Such learning is better caught than taught. A constant thought in our minds should be that our children are watching our example. Let us give them a chance. Let us give them a good example. Let us motivate them by the quality of our Christlike life.

Family Building

In *The Power of Maturity*, Louis Binstock tells this story:

> A wealthy man provided his family with all the comforts and luxuries that money can buy. Since he and his wife were busy with their social and business schedules, he made sure that their little boy and girl had a nurse and also a governess. The governess could have the use of the car and a chauffeur to take the children anywhere. If the children stayed home, they had every kind of toy and game to keep them happy, and a big swimming pool besides. The father, when he saw his

children now and then, beamed upon them and encouraged them to ask him for anything they wanted.

Then came a business reversal. The father went broke. Gone were the nurse and the governess and the chauffeur. The family had to move into a modest apartment. With no money to spend on entertaining and socializing, the parents had to stay home a great deal. This did not seem so bad since the whole family could be together. One night, parents and children were having a wonderful time, singing and laughing. Suddenly, the little girl, seated in her father's lap looked at him fondly and said, "Daddy, please don't ever be rich again."

How often do we hear parents lament over children who have gone astray, "But I gave them everything money could buy!" Yes—everything but themselves.

In *Adult Education in the Church*, edited by Roy B. Zuck and Gene A. Getz, Jeannette Acrea has a beautiful chapter entitled "Helping Parents Teach Christian Standards." She quotes Dr. Clyde M. Narramore in suggesting thirteen ways to help children grow spiritually:

1. *Establish a good relationship with your child.*

2. *Tell your child about your own experiences with God.*

3. *Talk with your child alone about his relationship to Christ.*
4. *Be sure your child attends a Bible-believing Sunday school and church.*
5. *Teach the Bible to your child.*
6. *Explain and interpret daily events in the light of the Bible.*
7. *Be an example of godliness to your child.*
8. *Flood your child's mind and heart with Christian literature.*
9. *Utilize music to influence your child.*
10. *Help your child develop Christian friendships.*
11. *Don't overlook the influence of Christian schools.*
12. *Christian camps can help your child.*
13. *Show your child how to share his faith with others.*

Make your child or children feel special. Plan occasional outings with each child alone. Family togetherness is fine and needed, but a child also needs to have a portion of his parents' time all to himself. Once in a while, give him a day or afternoon or even an hour that is all his.

Parent, your child is your most-prized possession! Though you gain the whole world—goods, fame, and the accolades of men—if you lose your children, you stand before God a failure. Build your fences. Build them wisely and fairly. Don't be afraid, in love, to use strict correction when the fences are crossed. You are rearing your child for God. Don't fail.

9

A WELL-BALANCED SOCIAL LIFE

One of the great challenges of young adulthood is developing a good, well-rounded social life. This is a critical time, a growing and maturing time; and friendships and social activities are very important.

Friendships

The writer of Proverbs tells us, "A man that hath friends must shew himself friendly: and there is a friend that sticketh closer than a brother" (Proverbs 18:24). In Proverbs 17:17 he says, "A friend loveth at all times, and a brother is born for adversity."

Young adulthood is a time of choosing friends. The early adult years can be lonely years for men as well as for women, especially if they are single. Most of the single young adult's friends of former days are married and wrapped up in family life, as are most of his business associates. These years, then, may be quite lonely until he finds new friends to fill the void. New friends tend to be persons with whom he shares common goals and interests.

Loneliness is not limited to single young adults. Many times the married young adult will experience loneliness as he thinks back and perhaps craves the friendships and activities of adolescence, since he is now tied down with a family and caring for young children. This loneliness has a tendency to disappear as the married or single young adult finds new friends, new hobbies, and new fulfillments for his interests.

The friends the young adult chooses are very important, for their influence is great. Friends influence by example, by word, and by peer pressure. We generally conform to our circle of friends simply because we want to be accepted. Almost irresistibly we tend to become like the friends with whom we associate. Unfortunately, in a close friendship the less worthy member is apt to draw the more worthy friend into his way of acting. This is why friendships should be carefully weighed and picked.

Edward F. Garesche, in his book *The Will to Succeed,* quotes a young man as saying, "I value my friends more than any other possession, and if I had to give up all my earthly possessions or sacrifice my friendships, I would keep the friendships."

This young man shows a great deal of wisdom and sense, for nothing in the world is of any more value than good, loving, close friends. Amos the

Prophet says, "Can two walk together, except they be agreed?" (Amos 3:3). The beauty of friendship and close companionship adds fulfillment to life. The young adult who has good, Christian friends is tremendously blessed.

Garesche further states:

True friendship is a beautiful thing. It is native to our human nature. The heart craves for friendship, and a generous heart is never satisfied until it is giving genuine friendship to others. But notice, that your friendship, by its very nature, can extend only to a comparatively few. The give and take of friendship, its effective sympathy and friendly intercourse, its exchange of opinions and convictions, its lively interest and serviceableness, demand that it be confined to a rather small circle, because no man is so powerful in his sympathies and so wide in his scope as to give real friendship to more than a limited number. We can be interested in a great many, be kindly to them, benefit them, but the duties of real friendship necessarily limits its sphere.

These facts make it all the more important for us to choose our friends well. Since they are our other self and a powerful influence in our life, the friends we make have much to do with our integrity, our nobleness of character and our true success.

Knowing their importance and value, the Christian young adult should chose his friends very carefully. His close friends should be traveling the same road of Holiness that he is and should be clinging to similar convictions and desires. Otherwise, the young adult will find himself in positions of compromising or even giving up convictions in order to go along with hastily chosen friends that are exerting a bad influence upon him.

The Bible gives some beautiful illustrations of the value of close friendships. They are like the salt that brings out the tastiness of a meal. Jonathan and David's friendship, portrayed in 1 Samuel 18:1-4; 23:16-18, is such an example. The Bible records that Jonathan loved David "as his own soul." This so beautifully shows the closeness of love of friends. This love was so great that Jonathan gave David his entire outfit, plus hunting and fighting apparel. Friendship is giving as well as receiving.

Among the many beautiful friendships recorded in the New Testament is the story of Paul's relationship to Priscilla and Aquila, whom Paul calls "my helpers" and who, he says, were so close to him that they "laid down their own necks" on Paul's behalf (Romans 16:3, 4).

Such is the quality and beauty of friendship. The Christian young adult must choose carefully his circle of close friends to be sure that his relationship with them will be the kind through which the presence of Jesus Christ might shine.

Elizabeth B. Hurlock, in *Developmental Psychology*, lists four characteristics about the young adult and his friends:

1. *Friends in adulthood are selected on the basis of congeniality.*

2. *The adult's personal friends are selected by the adult himself, and the relationship is a mutually satisfying one.*

3. *They usually have a small number of personal friends—three or four—because of their limited time for association with outsiders.*

4. *Most families have to determine the number of friends and the amount of entertaining from the amount of money they can afford and what is available for outside recreation.*

These are things that are considered by young adults as they determine their circle of friends. For the Christian young adult, the list should be enlarged. Several criteria should be considered in choosing friends:

1. *Does the person share my faith in Jesus Christ as Lord and Savior?*

2. *Will he have a tendency to draw me closer to or farther away from the Lord?*

3. *Do we have similar tastes and interests?*

4. *Are we able to afford the same activities?*
   One danger of friendships between persons of different financial abilities is that the one who has less financially may well find himself overextended from trying to keep up with his friends.

5. *Is he the kind of person I will enjoy spending my spare time with?*

6. *Can I feel free to express my feelings and be myself in all honesty and not be afraid of losing his friendship?*

7. *Will he relate well to my family? Will I feel free to take him home and introduce him, knowing there will be common acceptance?*

Popularity and Leadership

Everyone wants to be popular. The desire for acceptance and popularity through the adolescent years carries on over into the young adult years. Elizabeth B. Hurlock, in *Developmental Psychology,* says, "Of the many changes in social interests and activities the young adult must make, the major changes are in social groupings, popularity, and leadership."

It seems that the old adage "once a leader always a leader" holds true. Those who were leaders in high school seem to continue as the leaders through young adulthood. They become leaders in Jaycees, business clubs, service clubs, and the like.

However, the leader in adolescence does have some adjustment to make in young adulthood. He is the most likely to become a leader in his circle of friends and social groupings, but this more mature leadership does not come overnight. In the meantime, the one who was a leader in high school has a hard time becoming a follower in early young adulthood.

For example, as Hurlock points out, "The boy who was always the leader in high school and college due to being football hero, has a hard time adjusting when he gets to young adulthood and when leadership roles in business, industry, or community affairs go to men of higher socioeconomic status and prestige in the community than he has."

The young adult is, in a sense, beginning all over to prove his worth, his leadership ability, his ability to make a contribution of value and need. This can be frustrating unless the young adult realizes the situation and can channel his drives and abilities through lesser tasks and involvements until his ability is recognized and he is elevated to a leadership role.

Community Involvement

The Christian young adult faces the problem of whether or not he should become involved in community affairs. On the one hand, the introvert, believing in total and complete separation from the world, attempts to lock himself up in some little greenhouse of protection until Jesus comes. He has little or no contact with the world and wonders why he is spiritually barren, winning no one to the Lord. To the other extreme, the extrovert wants to join everything and be involved in everything until he has time for nothing at home, including family and God. Yet, there is a happy medium between these two positions.

Christians should let their influence be felt. Jesus called His people "the salt of the earth" (Matthew 5:13). Christians should give the world seasoning; but how can they if they never have any contact with the world? Christian influence, talent, and leadership ability should be felt in school-parents associations, service organizations, youth organizations, and community affairs. The young adult should look for doors where he might share his faith, either by word or by his vibrant Christian way of living.

Yet, most young adults draw back from community involvement. Thomas R. Bennett, writing in the December, 1965, issue of *International Journal of Religious Education,* says, "It is probably true to say that young adults tend to delay community participation until they have established a home and have children. The exception to this is among single persons in their late twenties, and among those with higher education and socioeconomic status."

Young adults need to be involved in the community. They have something to share; they have energy and enthusiasm to work; and, above all, God's people need to be making acquaintance with those whom they can share the good things of Jesus Christ.

Just beware to keep it in balance. Your relationships to family, God, and business come first. But do not neglect your opportunity to share with your neighbors in making your community a better place to live.

Church Life

There was a time, not too many years ago, when

life rotated around the church. Our friends were there, and our social as well as our spiritual life was wrapped up in the church. Unfortunately, our industrialized life-style and new moral and materialistic value system have caused us to lose that intimacy. It has been a great loss.

The more recent trend has been to the other extreme, with the church playing little or no part in our lives other than our attending an occasional service. Yet, we must allow the church to play a larger role in our life. Our closest friends should be the Christian friends with whom we worship.

The New Testament church had a very close communion, as is evidenced by the record in Acts 2. This close fellowship needs to be recaptured. We need not only to worship together with fellow Christians, but to play together in recreational and social activities and also to serve together in the community.

James defines our role as Christians when he says, "Pure religion and undefiled before God and the Father is this, To visit the fatherless and widows in their affliction, and to keep himself unspotted from the world" (James 1:27).

We must be in the world. We need to make our presence felt there. We need acquaintances and friends there. But, our close friendships should be with fellow brothers and sisters in the Lord.

The cry of the Gentile world of the New Testament was, "My, how they love one another!" That same cry should characterize the Church, the body of Christ, today. Such love, fellowship, and unity does not just happen on Sunday. It comes as lives are welded together through worship, work, fellowship, and fun throughout the week.

Jesus Christ is our example. The Bible calls Him the "friend that sticketh closer than a brother" (Proverbs 18:24). Our closest relationship is our relationship to Him.

God has a lot of children, but He doesn't have many who act like friends. Yet God calls Abraham and Lazarus His friends.

Our closest friendships should be with those who share our faith in God and with whom our relationship of "close friend" can be very Christ-centered. The attributes of Christ should be manifested in us. The love He shares with us we should share with others.

10

HANDLING FINANCES

The Bible has much to say about money. We read many stories in the Bible about people who had money problems, as well as other problems: the story of the Rich Young Ruler (Luke 18:18-25), the parable of the Rich Fool (Luke 12:16-21), and the parable of the Prodigal Son (Luke 15:11-32). All of these tell of people who did not own money, but rather, whose money owned them.

Probably one of the most misquoted verses in the Bible is 1 Timothy 6:10, where Paul says, "For the love of money is the root of all evil: which while some coveted after, they have erred from the faith, and pierced themselves through with many sorrows." Notice: Paul says that "the *love* of money," not *money* itself, is sin. Being wealthy is not wrong. Right or wrong comes in the way we use wealth.

Paul goes on in verse 11 to tell us not to seek

earnestly after money, but rather to seek after "righteousness, godliness, faith, love, patience, meekness." In other words, it is our priorities and motives that are important. Jesus said, "For where your treasure is, there will your heart be also" (Matthew 6:21).

Money is a necessary means of exchange in our society, and every young adult finds himself thrust into a world where success is judged by how much he has. The Christian young adult must learn to put all of this into perspective and must learn to be a good manager. All that we have is a gift of God. We are placed as stewards over the things God gives us; that is, we are only managers of the things that He has put into our care. Realizing this, we are aware of our Christian duty to use wisely and carefully everything that God has given us so that He can be glorified in it and so that we can be found faithful in using it for the sake of His kingdom.

Tackling Your Money Problems

Generally speaking, the urge for material possessions reaches its peak in young adulthood. Upon leaving adolescence most young people have dreams of the things they want out of life. They envision a nice car, a beautiful home, plenty of extras, the works. They become frustrated, however, if during their early adulthood, their job does not provide them the things they want. It is hard to think of planning ahead. The temptation is to think, *Mom and Dad have such and such things. Why can't I?* But Mom and Dad took twenty or thirty years to accumulate their possessions. Unfortunately, many young adults, not willing to wait and budget the family finances, charge too much, finance too much, and very soon find themselves swamped with installment payments they have a terrible time trying to meet. This often results in the husband taking a second job in the evenings, or the wife working. Generally, though, the lesson is not learned; past mistakes are not heeded; and in but a few short months, even with the wife working, the family again is financially strapped.

The home is a status symbol for young adults, and often they jeopardize the welfare of the family by trying to buy a home too soon and to furnish it with furniture more elaborate than their income really permits. Vance Packard, in his book *Status Seekers,* comments on why the home is such a status symbol for young adults:

> *The home during the late fifties began showing signs of supplanting the automobile as the status symbol most favored by Americans for staking their status claims. There are a number of explanations for this change, but the most important one, undoubtedly, is that with the general rise in incomes and installment buying a luxuriously sculptured chariot has become too easily obtainable for the great multitudes of status strivers. A home costs more money, a lot more. Another explanation is the appearance in profusion of mass merchandisers in the home-selling field,*

*who have become skilled . . . in surrounding
their product with status meanings. . . . Finally, visible signs of culture have their value in
conveying the impression of high status. . . .
One reason the home is replacing the auto-
mobile as a favored way for demonstrating
status is that a home can be a showcase for
"culture." In a home you can display an-
tiques, old glassware, leather-bound books,
classical records. These are things a car cannot do.*

This does not mean that homes have replaced
the car as a status symbol, but rather that young
adults have simply added it to the car as a more
impressive status symbol.

Much unhappiness is encountered in young
adulthood by those who have great dreams and
illusions of what they would like to attain, but then
find that, because of short finances, they cannot
afford such treasures while some of their closest
friends can.

The family may encounter much conflict over the
handling of the finances. The backgrounds of both
husband and wife before marriage have a large
bearing here. One spouse may have come from a
family where the father handled all the finances
and no one else knew anything about them, while
the other spouse may have come from a family
where the finances were a shared thing.

Agreeing on finances is more than agreeing on
a budget the family can live with. In the book
Adult Education in the Church, edited by Roy B.

Zuck and Gene A. Getz, W. J. Fields, in his chapter titled "Helping Families Maintain Marital Unity," says:

> *It also involves values and priorities. The wife may look at a new dress as a necessity, while the husband thinks of it as an unneeded luxury. On the other hand, he may feel a new set of golf clubs a necessity, while she feels like it is strictly in the unnecessary luxury class. She may want a freezer, while he thinks a new car should come first. All [these are] potential problem areas involving finances. So it becomes obvious that in marriage varying points of view are constantly in tension and must be worked out by making compromises and decisions.*

Too many young couples get into trouble because what they want they want *now*. They are not interested in planning and setting goals so that they can obtain large purchases later, at a time when it is within their budget. Sometimes it is difficult to realize that the future is important and that it is worth planning for.

No matter which spouse handles the money, communication should always be kept open so that both the husband and the wife are completely aware of the family's financial status. All money decisions should be made jointly. Far too many wives are left confused over finances they know nothing about and yet must handle because the husband is unexpectedly incapacitated. This ought not to be.

Managing Your Money

Judson T. and Mary G. Landis, in their book *Building a Successful Marriage*, say the first few years of marriage are "the time for learning to handle money wisely, establishing habits of financial responsibility, learning to cooperate in financial matters and determining what the two are willing to sacrifice for and what things are necessities that they must somehow manage to provide."

The family or the single young adult who puts off setting some guidelines for himself is inviting financial disaster. The basic financial problem for every family is to establish long-range economic goals. Without these goals for saving, spending, and budgeting, one can never really know where he is, where he is going, or how he is going to get there.

Ella M. Cushman, in *Management in Homes*, lists the following principles of home management:

1. *Have a goal.*
2. *Make a plan.*
3. *Face the obstacles.*
4. *Take stock of your resources and note possible ways to overcome obstacles.*
5. *Make investigations to get maximum value for your investments.*
6. *Experiment and test results whenever possible.*
7. *Act.*
8. *Evaluate the results.*

Most people do not obtain nice things by accident. Most middle-aged adults have a comfortable way of life because they began to plan for it in the young adult years. How? They set goals. They knew where they wanted to go. They knew how to get there.

Saving is one of the best means of planning ahead. Most financial counselors agree that persons should save at least 10 percent of their income. If young adults will start off planning to save at least 10 percent of their earnings, they will be able to obtain any goal they set.

There is another very important aspect to finances: giving to God. Far too many young adults get so strapped that they cannot give offerings or even pay their tithes. But we must remember this: everything we have or own is due to the blessings of God upon our lives. For us not to give God gifts of love and to pay our tithes is the height of self-ishness and unappreciativeness. By neglecting to do so, we are saying, "God, I am not thankful for what You have done." Many young adults are not prospering because of this.

Tithing is a command of God. Ten percent of what we earn is not ours, but God's. The Bible explicitly says, "The tithe . . . is the Lord's" (Leviticus 27:30).

Malachi 3:10 states, "Bring ye all the tithes into the storehouse." But in the same verse the writer, speaking for God, goes on and promises a blessing: "And prove me now herewith, saith the Lord of hosts, if I will not open you the windows of heaven, and pour you out a blessing, that there shall not be room enough to receive it." This verse should be considered along with Malachi 2:2, in which God says He will curse the blessings of those who refuse to obey Him.

Why do so many people struggle financially? Many have not learned the thrill and joy of giving to God and seeing how God will literally open heaven's windows to rain down blessings. The young adult who has learned that his first financial responsibility is his thank offering and tithe to God has learned the key to success.

Setting Up a Family Budget

Few people plan a budget and stick to it. Yet a budget is one of the most needed items in the family. To try and survive without one is like taking a 4,000-mile trip to a state where you have never been without a road map.

You need to decide where you want to go financially over the next few years and how you can distribute your income so that you may get the most for your money. Progress is possible after you reach this decision. Clearly defined goals reduce conflict and increase harmony within the family.

Good Housekeeping's Guide for Young Homemakers, compiled by the Good Housekeeping Institute, says, "A well-thought out budget should be one of the first matters to be tackled in a home. It is important to reconsider and to redraft if necessary this budget each year."

Making a budget can be very simple: First, the

family estimates what their income is or will be. Second, the family estimates what they want and need. (Since there will not always be enough money for all the wants, the family must subdivide its list into luxuries and necessities.) Third, they distribute their resources or income among the various items on the list.

Thus, we see that families need to keep records. They must know how much money they have to work with. They must know how and when they can spend. And, finally, they must plan their expenses and savings for the future.

Suggested percentages for a family's budget would approximate the following (according to some financial advisors): 20 percent for housing, 10 percent for savings, 20 percent for food, 10 percent for operating, 12 percent for clothes, 5 percent for medical expenses, 10 percent for church, 13 percent for extras.

There is no one method that is exactly right for every family. Each family will have to pray and seek the Lord's leading in choosing a budget that is best for them. However, some method of planned and organized financial record-keeping will be a must. A large percentage of family problems are concerned with money. The enemy tries every available means to discourage and harass God's people. Foolish and irresponsible financial activity opens a door for him to really work.

The Bible speaks often of stewards or managers. We are to be good stewards. God has given blessings to each of us. It is our responsibility to make the most of those blessings.

Be careful of the way you spend and use your money. Be extremely careful of credit. Used carefully and advisedly, credit can be a great help; used unwisely, it can be a serious threat to the harmony and unity of the family. If you have to buy something on time, understand the method of operation of the agency extending the credit and the exact rate of interest. Or, better yet, pay cash for everything you possibly can. This is where a good savings program is helpful.

Matthew 10 relates the charge Jesus gave the Twelve before He sent them forth to minister. He told them to "be . . . wise as serpents" (verse 16). Nowhere is this admonition anymore needed than in the realm of family finances. Much discouragement, frustration, futility, and sleeplessness can be avoided if the family will proceed cautiously and prayerfully in this area of family life.

Perhaps another injunction of Jesus is appropriate here: "Seek ye first the kingdom of God, and his righteousness; and all these things shall be added unto you" (Matthew 6:33). Remember: God's children are Kingdom-seekers, not status-seekers

11

DEVELOPING A
VIBRANT FAITH IN GOD

Louis Binstock, in *The Power of Maturity*, tells
the following story:

> In the early nineteenth century, in the
> small village of Hanipol, in eastern Europe,
> there lived a great teacher named Zusya. He
> was a leader of the Jewish sect, the Hasidim,
> which chose the mystical rather than the
> rational approach to God. Attempting to solve
> the divine mystery, they searched for the
> formula for the ideal man. Thus they might
> be able to follow the Biblical commandment:
> "Ye shall be perfect even as I, the Lord your
> God, am perfect." Zusya had chosen as his
> model the great Moses, God's most trusted
> servant. But after many years of profound
> study and community service, Zusya felt he

*was still as far below the peak of Moses'
towering character as was the village of
Hanipol below the peaks of the surrounding
mountains.*

*One night exhausted, he fell asleep, and
God appeared to him in a dream. "Why are
you so disturbed, my son?" asked God. "You
have climbed high on the ladder of perfection."*

*"Owed," Zusya whispered, "But my days on
earth will soon be ended, and I must climb so
much higher to make myself like Moses."*

*Smiling, God answered, "Worry no more.
When you appear before my throne of judgment, I will not ask 'Why were you not like
Moses?' I will ask, 'Why were you not Zusya,
your possible self?' You are not expected to
reach the perfection of Moses. You are expected to fulfill the fullest potential of Zusya,
yourself."*

Whether or not it is a true story is not important; the message is. Too many people are trying
desperately to copy someone else's life and, in thus
doing, hope to find success and meaning. God has
not called us to be anyone but ourselves. He
created us, and makes no mistakes. It is as one
poor young man stated, in stressing his worth de-
spite meager surroundings, "God made me, and
He don't make no trash!"

We have an obligation to be perfect. Matthew
5:48 says, "Be ye therefore perfect, even as your
Father which is in heaven is perfect." Much mis-

interpretation has arisen over the word *perfect*. In the Greek it simply means "mature."

The Christian growth in life very much parallels the physical life. We start as a baby and slowly, gradually mature into adults. God's children are expected to mature. This does not happen overnight, nor does it ever stop; it is a continual process. In Hebrews 6:1 the writer says, "Let us leave behind the elementary teachings of Christ, and advance toward maturity" (*Berkeley*). We spend too much time in the past, talking about things we have already experienced and growth we have already attained. Let us move on into deeper things in God and mature in our walk of Christlikeness. This is an important part of the young adult years.

Much is said about the terrible trauma and all of the hardships and pressures of the teenage years. It is a very trying time, but the fact is that the young adult years are a far more treacherous time. Many persons, upon finally reaching adulthood, are ready to retreat into the haven they had as teens. Yet, in the midst of all the pressures, the pulls, and the adjustments, the young adult must find himself and evaluate who he is, where he is, and where he is going. This evaluation must occur on every level: spiritual, vocational, and social. It is only by taking an honest look inward that he can begin moving forward in the maturing process.

Looking Inward

Binstock, quoted earlier, says:

Before you can conquer yourself, you must know yourself. Take a real hard look at the inner you. Like an iceberg, most of it floats invisibly below the surface. Only a small part of you shows above the surface. It presents the picture you wish to portray to others. It is your public image on parade. If you are clever, you'll make sure that people like your public image, while only you may know what you are like underneath. . . . The mature person is conscious of his strength as well as his weaknesses and he backs up his own strengths. What he knows, he knows well. Where he is particularly capable, he knows it, and does not envy another person who, in the same field, may be even more capable.

The mature person sees too that a weakness in one direction need not take away from a strength in another direction. The horse cannot fly like a bird; but, then, a bird cannot pull a wagon.

We would agree that this is looking at maturity from a human standpoint. However, the basics are still true. Although we, as Christians, have turned our lives over to the Lord Jesus Christ as Lord and Savior, we are not perfect in every way. There still is a daily growing in Christlikeness. Natural babies do not become men and women in a week, and neither do babes in Christ. There is a growing process that never stops. To stop growing is to die. This is evidenced by the number of spiritual corpses on church pews.

The Christian has a source to help him in the maturing process that the non-Christian does not have. The non-Christian goes it alone, trying to be better, trying to change, trying to mature, but failing. The Christian has the power through the Holy Spirit dwelling within him to be led and directed more perfectly in his walk of growing and maturing into Christlikeness. As the Christian yields himself to Christ, the Holy Spirit can do a work in his life.

This is not to say the Christian does none of the work. First of all, he must yield to God's working; second, he must do what he can to live as Christ directed. (This is dealt with more in the next chapter.) Christians need to look in the mirror and honestly evaluate themselves. They need to take a good look inside and see if Jesus Christ really is Lord of all, or if there are harbored thoughts, attitudes, and desires that are hidden like the iceberg. Maturity is looking at ourselves, seeing the childish parts of our lives, and being willing to grow.

Edward F. Garesche, in *The Will to Succeed,* says:

It requires plenty of real courage and honesty to be sincere with oneself. There are many men and women who, their whole lives long, are afraid to stand face to face with their own mistakes and with the defects of their own character. They deceive themselves about themselves. They actually contrive, in spite of daily experience, to remain blind to their own faults and shortcomings.

A most dangerous deception is self-deception.
It is only by seeing ourselves as we are that
we can remake and perfect our own charac-
ter.

Certainly, for the Christian, the realization is
that self-evaluation must be done with the power
and leadership of God.

Growing to Maturity

What is maturity? It is not a state of being, but
a state of becoming. Adults are not "grown-up,"
but rather "growing up."

Maturity is, in some respects, what the Bible
refers to as wisdom. In the Old Testament, the
word *wisdom* denoted a skill or an ability in living. Knowing how to live, how to make decisions,
and how to choose wisely was maturity.

Maturity is one criterion of adulthood, but unfortunately it has nothing at all to do with age or
size. A child of six may be wiser by far than his
years, while an adult of sixty may have lived his
life childishly and immaturely.

Louis Binstock, in *The Power of Maturity*,
quotes Dr. McMurray, head of a leading personal
counseling agency, as listing ten signs of immaturity:

1. To seek and use money or material things
   as ends in themselves—not merely as
   means towards those ends.
2. To accord pleasure undue importance.
3. To live only for the immediate present.

4. To commit yourself to a world of fantasy. Many children live lives rich in fantasy, as is well known. But what is not well known is the fact that this is also a characteristic of many adults.
5. To behave as if you were all-powerful.
6. To be a show-off.
7. To have no self-control.
8. To dodge the acceptance of blame.
9. To become too dependent on independence.
10. To be a mistake blotter; to refuse to learn by experience so we won't repeat the same mistakes again.

Binstock then counters with ten pillars of maturity:

1. A sense of reality
2. The quality of flexibility
3. A reasonable feeling of independence
4. Willingness to accept responsibility
5. Enthusiastic confidence in oneself
6. Self-discipline (self-control)
7. Decisiveness of purpose
8. An abundance of love
9. Patience and the courage to be patient
10. The light of hope

Yet maturity cannot be complete unless it has as its foundation a vibrant faith in the Lord Jesus Christ. He is the rock, the foundation of life and of living. A person cannot comprehend the potential and worth of life unless he is being guided in his maturity by the Holy Spirit.

Experiencing a Vibrant Faith

It has been noted that the early twenties are the least religious period of life. During these years there is a noticeable decrease in church attendance and indifference to other religious observances. This is usually not reversed until parenthood responsibilities are assumed and the young adult again feels the necessity of church involvement. Certainly, there are many young adults who keep a vibrant faith during this time. However, just as certainly, the majority do not.

The young adult needs a vibrant faith in God. During the times of terrible pressure from obtaining an education, starting a career, and beginning a family, faith in God is of utmost help. Dag Hammarskjold, in his book *Markings,* has an entry dated 1952 which reads, "What I ask for is absurd: that life shall have a meaning. What I strive for is impossible: that my life shall acquire a meaning." A meaning for life is perhaps impossible outside of Jesus; but when one has established a firm faith in God, life does have meaning and purpose. Edna St. Vincent Millay in one of her poems says:

> *Life must go on;*
> *I forget just why.*

This echoes the feelings of a lot of empty, disillusioned people in the world. But the "why" of life is Jesus Christ. He is why we live, and He is life! Jesus said, "Without me ye can do nothing" (John 15:5). The young adult needs to learn that. Christianity is not for the very young and the very old; it is a vibrant experience for all, needed when we have to face the trials of life. And there is no greater time of need for divine help and guidance than during the years of young adulthood.

Young adults get weary. To such Jesus said, "Come unto me, all ye that labour and are heavy laden, and I will give you rest" (Matthew 11:28). Young adults often feel lonely, but Jesus said, "Lo, I am with you alway, even unto the end of the world" (Matthew 28:20). Young adults are pressured by a very loose society where anything goes, but Jesus said, "If ye shall ask any thing in my name, I will do it" (John 14:14).

This kind of vibrant faith does not come easy. Satan fights every step of the way. (We will talk about dealing with the way he works in the following chapter.) But because he is already a defeated foe, we should press on in Christlike living.

How does a vibrant faith in God come? First, it takes desire. A person does not normally stumble into a close relationship with God. He must want it to happen. The Bible says, "Desire the sincere milk of the word, that ye may grow thereby" (1 Peter 2:2). Desire it. Want it. Covet it. That is the only way to obtain it.

After one has a desire, he must seek it. The things of God are not just dumped on us; neither do we have to necessarily work for or earn them. But we must desire them and seek them.

Be assured that you are promised a vibrant faith.

Rest confidently in the knowledge that God wants you to have it. Then press on and seek it.

The little lady with the issue of blood was convinced that Jesus would heal her, but she did not wait around. She went to find Him (Luke 8:43, 44). Jacob knew there was a blessing for him, and he fought all night, refusing to let go until he received it (Genesis 32:24-32). David knew God would defeat Goliath, but he went out and confidently threw the stone (1 Samuel 17:40-50). The four men with a sick friend knew Jesus would help, so they tore the roof apart in order to get through the multitude to the feet of Jesus (Luke 5:17-26). And on and on through the Word the list goes.

When Michael Faraday, the great scientist, lay dying a friend asked him, "What are your speculations?"

Gently Faraday replied, "Speculations? I have none. I rest my soul on certainties."

The young adult who begins early to build his life on Jesus Christ as the sure foundation will save himself much heartache and disappointment. There is nothing as comforting as to be aware of the sound of sandaled footsteps walking beside us.

Binstock quotes a portion from Eugene O'Neill's play *More Stately Mansions* which says:

> *When I was about 17, a large apartment building began to go up across the street from where I lived, and within a month or two the depression struck. Halfway up to its promised six or seven stories, with brick-work rising at*

*irregular heights and with windows marked
like the teeth in a jack-o-lantern, the building stopped. No men came back to work; no
money was ever found to put the flooring into the vast cavity. And every day I passed
newness that was turning into oldness without having once been used. In due time,
three or four years later, the world began to
move again and with this movement came the
wreckers. Nothing could be salvaged; not the
wings that met at rectangles, not the stone
that framed a court yard, not the blind in-
tricate foundations that scurried maze-like,
unidentified and uncrowned, inside the shell.
I always felt wistful about that building.*

This doesn't just happen with buildings. There
are also many people standing around uncom-
pleted. They lack the vibrant faith in God that
gives completeness to life. They go on unused,
short of potential, lacking in meaning, and empty
of satisfaction.

The young adult needs to survey his life, to look
inside, and to ask himself, "Am I what I ought to
be? Do I have any real meaning and peace in
life? Have I built my life on the firm foundation
found in Jesus Christ? or on the corroding values
of the world?" If the answer is not pleasing, then
he needs to do something about it.

"If any man thirst, let him come unto me, and
drink. He that believeth on me, as the scripture
hath said, out of his belly shall flow rivers of
living water" (John 7:37, 38).

12

DEALING WITH THE DEVIL

I have given them thy word; and the world hath hated them, because they are not of the world, even as I am not of the world. I pray not that thou shouldest take them out of the world, but that thou shouldest keep them from the evil (John 17:14, 15).

And these are they by the way side, where the word is sown; but when they have heard, Satan cometh immediately, and taketh away the word that was sown in their hearts (Mark 4:15).

And the Lord said, Simon, Simon, behold, Satan hath desired to have you, that he may sift you as wheat: But I have prayed for thee, that thy faith fail not: and when thou art converted, strengthen thy brethren (Luke 22:31, 32).

It is a simple fact: if we love God, we are at

war with the devil. We have no choice in the matter. Satan hates God's children and is intent on making life miserable for them and hopefully shaking their faith. He will harass, tempt, oppress, discourage, and do any other thing possible to beat us down.

Who Satan Is

We must realize that we are in a battle and we are the prize. Peter writes, "Be sober, be vigilant; because your adversary the devil, as a roaring lion, walketh about, seeking whom he may devour" (1 Peter 5:8). Paul tells us the scope of this battle by describing our enemies in Ephesians 6:12: "For we wrestle not against flesh and blood, but against principalities, against powers, against the rulers of the darkness of this world, against spiritual wickedness in high places."

Satan has declared war on God and His children. Realizing this, we need to know how he operates. Before a general takes his army into battle, he learns everything he can about the enemy, so that he will be better equipped strategically to fight him. The Christian would be wise to do the same. He should learn all he can, through Scripture, concerning the enemy. Then he should arm himself for battle.

How Satan Works

Satan knows all the tricks. He is a master deceiver and liar, as evidenced by the way the Bible

shows him tempting Eve and others. But let us remember: he is a liar. If he tells us that doing a
certain thing will be all right, let us rest assured
it will turn out all wrong. Satan has a lot of apples.
They are bright and shiny and look delicious. But,
we should be assured: all Satan's apples have
worms. King David could confirm this by telling
the results of his yielding to Satan's lure.

If we are going to resist the devil, then we must
know how he works. Satan appeals to the flesh.
James tells us, "But every man is tempted, when he
is drawn away of his own lust, and enticed. Then
when lust hath conceived, it bringeth forth sin:
and sin, when it is finished, bringeth forth death.
Do not err, my beloved brethren" (James 1:14-
16). Let us notice the pattern; it is always the
same: lust, sin, spiritual death. *Lust* is "a driving
desire to possess or have something." Satan plays
on this.

Satan works very hard on our minds and bodies. He appeals to the natural drives and emotions.
These drives that God has created within us—and
also for which He has given proper and pure out-
lets—Satan will try to pollute and use wrongly.
Whenever we feel tempted to do anything that
does not coincide with God's Word, we should recognize it as Satan's lure. Paul, writing in 2 Corinthians 2:11, says, "We are not ignorant of his
[Satan's] devices." Nor should we be. Too many
Christians get tripped up and have problems because they do not realize—until it is too late—
how their archenemy works.

Satan will work on our minds by creating thoughts that should not be there. Feelings of hurt, hatred, malice, and greed are not from God. Satan will fill our minds with trash and garbage unless we refuse to allow it.

Whatever is given credence in our thinking will eventually wind up in our heart. Satan might throw a thought at us that we should not have. If we allow it to linger and dwell upon it, it will grow. It eventually will take root in our heart as lust or hatred or some other equally damaging feeling.

Again, we see the pattern developing of which James speaks: lust, sin, and death. We who refuse to defend ourselves and accept God's promised victory in these areas of life are playing with spiritual death! Satan has thousands of years of experience on us. He knows all the tricks, and he has used them many times. He is a master at deceiving, lying, and tempting. Trying to handle his onslaughts ourselves or trying to ignore the problem will never bring victory. But victory is ours in Jesus Christ!

Who We Are

The sixteenth chapter of the Gospel of John records a beautiful picture of Jesus with the disciples as He was teaching them and trying to prepare them for what He knew was just ahead: His death. He told them they would soon be scattered, and then He made a surprising statement: "Be of good cheer; I have overcome the world" (verse 33).

Here was a Man who, from the natural standpoint, had nothing. He owned nothing but the clothes on His back. His disciples ate from the fields as they passed through. His ministry had lasted three years, and He had only twelve men with Him to carry on. These twelve still did not understand fully what He was teaching, and one of them was soon to betray Him.

Yet, in the midst of what seemed to be total defeat, He made a beautiful confession of victory. You see, He was not looking at circumstances around Him, but rather at the final victory just a few days ahead. He knew the victory was His.

We too share in that victory. In Romans 8:37-39 Paul says:

> *Nay, in all these things we are more than conquerors through him that loved us. For I am persuaded, that neither death, nor life, nor angels, nor principalities, nor powers, nor things present, nor things to come, Nor height, nor depth, nor any other creature, shall be able to separate us from the love of God, which is in Christ Jesus our Lord.*

Then to the Ephesians Paul says:

> *And what is the exceeding greatness of his power to us-ward who believe, according to the working of his mighty power, Which he wrought in Christ, when he raised him from the dead, and set him at his own right hand in the heavenly places, Far above all principality, and power, and might, and dominion, and every name that is named, not only*

*in this world, but also in that which is to
come: And hath put all things under his feet,
and gave him to be the head over all things
to the church, Which is his body, the fulness
of him that filleth all in all* (Ephesians 1:19-
23).

All things have been put under His feet. All
power, all authority, all victory has been given to
Jesus Christ, the head of the Body. Every person
who accepts Jesus Christ as his personal Savior becomes a member of the body of Christ, to whom
He delegated all His power and authority. In Mark
16:15-20, we see, He sent His followers out, as
He still does us today, with the power and the
authority to exercise His name over evil and un-
clean spirits. And His name has power. Demons
fall and retreat at the power of His name.

We are the victors, because as members of His
body, we have a right to use His name. John reminds us, in John 14:12-15, that the works done
by Jesus are still being done by His body. Jesus
Christ won victory over Satan, death, hell, and the
grave. He passed that victory on to us. We are
not struggling, barely-getting-along Christians, but
rather victors in Christ Jesus. The devil knows that,
but he does not want us to know it.

Knowing that Satan works on our minds and on
our bodies, we have the responsibility to do something about it. We are the victors in Christ Jesus,
so we must stand against the enemy's attacks. The
devil will have a heyday with our minds if we don't
resist him.

How? The Word tells us emphatically in Philippians 2:5, "Let this mind be in you, which was also in Christ Jesus." That is a frightening statement. We are to have the same mind, desires, direction, purpose, and attitudes as Christ had.

"Impossible!" you say? Yet, the Bible tells us how: by renewing our minds. Paul writes, "And be renewed in the spirit of your mind" (Ephesians 4:23). In Colossians 3:16 he says, "Let the word of Christ dwell in you richly in all wisdom." And then in Romans 12:1, 2 he states:

> *I beseech you therefore, brethren, by the mercies of God, that ye present your bodies a living sacrifice, holy, acceptable unto God, which is your reasonable service. And be not conformed to this world: but be ye transformed by the renewing of your mind, that ye may prove what is that good, and acceptable, and perfect, will of God.*

Or, as the J. B. Phillips translation says, "Don't let the world around you squeeze you into its own mold" (verse 2).

We renew our mind on the Word of God. The Holy Spirit anoints the Word and prepares our hearts to receive its message. The Word becomes milk and meat to us spiritually, and we grow thereby.

Many Christians have battles here because they do not know what the Word of God says. They do not realize that they are victors, because they don't know the Word tells them they are.

There is power in the Word. Jesus used the

Word to resist the temptations of the devil in the wilderness. We, too, should resist temptations with the Word of God. But how can we, if we have not read the Word enough to let it renew our mind day by day and dwell richly in our heart? We can't.

The second area of Paul's admonition in Romans 12:1, 2 deals with Satan's attack on our bodies. Paul tells us to bring our bodies into subjection. Our body is not eternal; our spiritual man is. At death our body goes into a grave; our spirit and soul go to be with the Lord. The problem is this: we can live our Christian life two ways. Our physical man, with all of its desires and drives, can govern us and keep us in misery; or, our spiritual man can be in control, leading us into a Christlike life. This is the battle Paul speaks of in Romans 7:19, 20. This warfare is constantly going on as to who will rule our life: the physical man or the spiritual man. This, then, is why Paul says, in Romans 12:1, that we are to bring our body into subjection. We must make sure that the inner man —the hidden man of the heart, the spiritual man —is in control and that everything else is in subjection to him.

How We Work

Victory is ours. It was won for us through Calvary and an empty tomb. Jesus Christ defeated the enemy, won victory, and then gave us the power and the authority to use His name so we could continue to defeat the devil as well. But it is up to us.

James 4:7 says, "Submit yourselves therefore to

God. Resist the devil, and he will flee from you."
The verse does not say the devil will flee from Jesus; it does not say he will flee from the preacher;
but it says he will flee from us. We must take a
stand and defeat him when he comes at us or our
family. As Christians we have the right to use the
name of Jesus. So, let us use it freely, for in it is all
the power we need to keep our enemy at bay.

Peter, writing in 1 Peter 5:9, tells us the same
thing: "Resist [the devil] stedfast in the faith."
Again, it is up to us. We must resist him.

Timothy is encouraged by Paul in 1 Timothy
6:12 to "fight the good fight of faith." It is a battle, a real battle. Many Christians let Satan win by
default. They just do not try to fight. And they
still wonder why they live such a defeated life.
The reason is obvious: they are not claiming the victory promised by Jesus, nor are they standing in the
faith and using the weapons God has given them.

Paul enumerates our weapons in Ephesians 6:
13-17. If we observe the list closely, we will notice that the Christian is really outfitted to fight the
enemy. There is only one place unprotected: the
back. The unwritten rule then is, "Do not retreat.
Stay in the battle. Keep the faith. Win the victory."
It already belongs to you—in the name of Jesus.

Paul tells us in Colossians 1:13 that we have already been delivered from the powers of darkness.
Satan knows that, but he doesn't give up. It is only
as we stand and defeat him that we will claim the
victory and that he will be reminded of the power
of the Lord.

Paul, in Ephesians 5:14, says, "Awake thou that sleepest." There is a message here for each of us. Satan has lulled the body of Christ to sleep. Most Christians are living mediocre lives that are tasteless, rather than salty. They are downtrodden; they do not share the victory of Christ; and they are doing nothing about it. Let us wake up! Victory is ours! Let us stand up, fight in the name of Jesus, defeat the enemy, and receive the victory.

"What shall we then say to these things? If God be for us, who can be against us?" (Romans 8:31).

Lord, make me a nail
Fastened securely in its place.
Then from this thing so common and so small
Hang a bright picture of Thy face,
That travelers may pause to look upon
The loveliness depicted there.
And traveling on their wearied ways
Each radiant face may bear,
Stamped so that nothing can efface
The image of Thy glory and Thy grace.
Lord, let not one soul think of me
Only let me be
A mark upon the wall
Holding Thy picture in its place.

13

MINISTERING TO YOUNG ADULTS

Knowing that young adults have specific needs, pressures, and problems is one thing; doing something about it is another. The church must acquaint itself with young adults and their needs.

H. Norman Wright, writing in *Ways to Help Them Learn (Adult)*, says:

> For the most part young adults are urban and mobile. They are very independent and are searching for something new. They don't always know what they are searching for, but they want life to be different and better than what they have seen in the previous generation. They react against the impersonalism of being lost in a crowd, yet they are still a part of this life style.
>
> The values of the past generation are not binding upon young adults. They hesitate to take what they are told at face value, espe-

*cially if it comes from institutions and those
who represent their "growing up" world. In a
sense they are attempting to carve out their
own world with its own customs, values and
beliefs, yet still retain some remnant of the
past world.*

These issues and feelings must be dealt with.
Young adults will not blindly respond to demands
such as, "Do it because the church says so." The
church must be prepared to back up its remarks
with Scripture when young adults ask, "Why?"

To minister to young adults, we must understand them. Young adulthood is not just a fad or a
brief ailment to be gotten over. Rather, as Allen J.
Moore says in *Introduction to Christian Education,*
edited by Marvin J. Taylor, "It is an era: a time
in which certain important events and happenings
are taking place within a person." These twelve to
fifteen years in a person's life are crucial to him.
The church must be a help.

Mr. Moore quotes from studies by the Methodist
Young Adult Research Project which clarified some
of the developmental questions or issues of the
young adult era. The following observations were
made:

1. Self-definition vs. Vagueness
   Young adults want to know, "Who am I?"
   How is this "I" going to be expressed in
   life?
2. Belonging vs. Isolation
   Belonging is the ability to give oneself
   and to receive another.

3. Maturity vs. Regression
   Maturity is growing in one's ability to assume responsibility for the various aspects of human life.
4. Meaning vs. Confusion
   A person only really lives as he finds an organized body of meaning that gives significance to life. To fail to find meaning leaves life in confusion.
5. Spontaneity vs. Rigidity
   A young adult learns to be free from his impulses and free from stereotype behaviors. He wants to be caught in the alive now rather than the dead past.

These are some of the issues young adults are facing. Is the church meeting these needs? Not very well.

Where the Church Has Failed

Most churches will admit that the greatest deficiency in their program is found in their ministry to young adults. Statistics show us that 70 percent of the population is urban, and the percentage is growing. Yet, 70 percent of the churches of fourteen major denominations are town and country.

Young adults who come to the city find a multitude of other interests to fill their busy schedule; hence, their move to the city is marked by decreased church attendance. This is due, according to Mr. Moore, to the fact that rural churches do not prepare young adults for city life, and the city churches do not absorb the newly arrived young adults into their program.

This is further proven by interviews with 421 young adults, according to Thomas R. Bennett, in the December, 1965, issue of *International Journal of Religious Education.* These interviews, among other things, showed the importance and centrality of friendship during this time of life.

> *Among the married, 9 out of 10 indicated that their homes were central meeting places. Schools, taverns and bars, drive ins, and bowling alley's were important meeting places for single young adults. Less than 10%, either single or married, mentioned the church as a place to meet with friends. . . .*
>
> *Many patterns of adult programs and activities are not congenial to young adults. Much the church provides is organizational-centered and formal. The recreational activities of young adults are centered in the home and with friends. For both single and married persons, the top two choices of free-time activities were 'friends and conversation' and 'watching T.V.' Among the lowest-ranking activities were 'belonging to organizations' and 'attending meetings.'*
>
> *One wonders, therefore, what would happen for the young adults and for the building of Christian lives and families if the church should attempt more in their homes and should accept their interests as the definition of its program.*

One of the real failures of the church has been its ministry to the family. Dr. Kenneth O. Gangel, in *The Family First,* says, "The church hasn't helped the situation. Rather than seeking to mold the family back into a functioning unit, the church often schedules programs several nights in the week, each drawing the attention of one or two family members and leaving the rest at home. In our harried effort to live by the clock, we have confused programs with productivity, meetings with meaning, and success with spirituality." It does not have to be this way. The church must reach the vast young adult populace of the country.

What the Church Can Do

The church cannot afford to ignore any longer the needs of young adults. It must gear itself and train itself to minister to them. This will take effort, self-study, and training. But these are long overdue anyway.

Allen Moore, quoted earlier, says, "No relevant ministry can occur until the church learns to see beneath the surface of young adult behavior, some cf which may even be deplorable, and to recognize the deeper signs of an intense struggle for meaning and selfhood."

In order to minister to young adults, the church must strive to understand them. This also includes understanding the world in which they are living and the pressures that they are facing. The church must view them, as one writer characterized them, as "liberated, skeptical, and searching." They are looking for meaning, peace, direction, and purpose.

Why is the church afraid to reach out to them, to go after them? We have in Christ Jesus, if we possess what we profess, the answer to their every need. Jesus said, "I am the way" (John 14:6). He also said, "Come unto me . . . and I will give you rest" (Matthew 11:28). Proverbs 3:5, 6, says, "Trust in the Lord with all thine heart; and lean not unto thine own understanding. In all thy ways acknowledge him, and he shall direct thy paths."

Ronald W. Johnson, writing in the September, 1966, issue of *International Journal of Religious Education,* tells how his church is ministering to young adults: "Our planning committee of six young adults is trying to ask and to answer very realistically two questions: 'What are the needs of young adults. . . .?' and 'How can our church serve these needs?' From answers to these basic questions, many experimental programs are starting."

The church needs to evaluate the needs of young adults and then strive to help meet those needs. We have discussed throughout the book some of the developmental tasks of young adults. Many young adults do not know how to accomplish these tasks. The church should offer programs and learning experiences that will show young adults how to meet them—not through learning for learning's sake, but through learning for humanity's sake. Young adults need to be taught how to participate in society and to understand how a Christian relates to and lives in the world. Then they need to be shown how to apply what they have been taught.

We do not stand still. We grow, or we regress. The young adult has much to learn. Why should he turn to the secular world to learn it? He should turn to the church to learn the skills of living. The fact that young adults are not turning to the church is evidence that the church is not meeting their needs.

One of the best ways of helping young adults is simply listening. Many churches are doing things in this realm. Small groups are meeting once a week in a home to study a book of the Bible chapter by chapter and to interact on it as they go. Listening groups are meeting once or twice a month to practice the art of listening and to learn to communicate and share openly and honestly. Churches are renting beach houses for the summer so that each Saturday the young adults can have a time of recreation, topped off with an extended rap session. Other churches are offering elective Sunday school classes on young adult needs. Your church can do something too!

The church must reach young adults—we cannot say that enough! We must go with them to school, to the armed forces, to work, and to the apartment. We must love them, minister to them, and help them. Jesus, in a parable, said, "Go out into the highways and hedges, and compel them to come in" (Luke 14:23). Jesus told the church, "Go . . . and teach" (Matthew 28:19). Yet, the church has been shouting, "Come and hear!" People are not coming, so perhaps we should start going!

BIBLIOGRAPHY

Bennett, Thomas R. "A Profile of the Young Adult." *International Journal of Religious Education* (December, 1965).

Bergevin, Paul. *A Philosophy for Adult Education*. New York: Seabury, 1967.

Binstock, Louis. *The Power of Maturity*. New York: Hawthorn, 1969.

Burnham, Helen A., Evelyn G. Jones, and Helen D. Redford. *Boys Will Be Men*. New York: Lippincott, 1942.

Chamberlin, J. Gordon. *The Church and Its Young Adults*. New York: Abingdon-Cokesbury, 1943.

Christenson, Larry. *The Christian Family*. Minneapolis: Bethany Fellowship, 1970.

Cushman, Ella M. *Management in Homes*. New York: Macmillan, 1945.

Dobson, James. *Dare to Discipline*. Wheaton, Ill.: Tyndale, 1970.

Feucht, Oscar E., ed. *Helping Families Through the Church*. St. Louis: Concordia, 1957.

Gangel, Kenneth O. *The Family First*. Minneapolis: HIS, 1972.

Garesche, Edward F. *The Will to Succeed*. New York: Kennedy, 1931.

Hammarskjold, Dag. *Markings*. Westminster, Md.: Knopf, 1964.

Hanson, Joseph John. *Our Church Plans for Young Adults*. Valley Forge: Judson, 1962.

Havighurst, Robert J. *Human Development and Education*. New York: McKay, 1953.

Hendrix, Olan. *Management and the Christian Worker*. Kilpauk, Madras: HBI, 1970.

Hill, Napoleon. *Think and Grow Rich*. New York: Hawthorn, 1966.

Howe, Reuel L. *The Creative Years*. New York: Seabury, 1959.

Hurlock, Elizabeth B. *Developmental Psychology*. New York: McGraw-Hill, 1959.

Johnson, Ronald W. "A Ministry to Young Adults in the City." *International Journal of Religious Education* (September, 1966).

Laas, William, *et al*, ed. *Good Housekeeping's Guide for Young Homemakers*. New York: Harper and Row, 1966.

Landis, Judson T. and Mary G. *Building a Successful Marriage*. Englewood Cliffs, N. J.: Prentice-Hall, 1963.

Maurois, Andre. *The Art of Living*. New York: Harper and Row, 1959.

Packard, Vance. *The Status Seekers*. New York: McKay, 1959.

Prince, Derek. "Fatherhood (Part I)." *New Wine* (April, 1974).

——————. "Fatherhood (Part II)." *New Wine* (May, 1974).

Raines, Margaret. *Managing Livingtime*. Peoria, Ill.: Bennett, 1964.

Sherrill, Lewis Joseph. *The Struggle of the Soul*. New York: Macmillan, 1963.

Super, Donald E. *The Psychology of Careers*. New York: Harper and Row, 1957.

Taylor, Marvin J., ed. An Introduction to Christian Education. New York: Abingdon, 1966.

Trueblood, Elton. *Your Other Vocation*. New York: Harper and Row, 1952.

Wright, H. Norman. *Ways to Help Them Learn (Adult)*. Glendale, Calif.: International Center for Learning, 1971.

Zeigler, Earl F. *Christian Education of Adults*. Philadelphia: Westminster, 1958.

Zuck, Roy B., and Gene A. Getz, eds. *Adult Education in the Church*. Chicago: Moody, 1970.